CISSP Fast Track

Master CISSP Essentials for Exam Success

Exam Cram Notes

1st Edition

Table of Contents

VERSAtile Reads

Chapter 01: How to Become a CISSP

Introduction

In today's digital age, where cyber threats are widespread, the demand for skilled information security professionals has never been higher. Among the many certifications available, the Certified Information Systems Security Professional (CISSP) stands out as a symbol of expertise and proficiency in cybersecurity. This chapter aims to guide you through the process of obtaining CISSP certification, offering valuable insights and practical tips to help you attain this esteemed credential.

What is a CISSP?

CISSP stands for Certified Information Systems Security Professional. It is a globally recognized certification offered by the International System Security Certification Consortium, also known as (ISC)². CISSP is widely regarded as one of the most esteemed certifications in the fields of information security and cybersecurity. Individuals pursue CISSP certification to meet the demand for experienced and highly capable IT professionals who can effectively oversee an enterprise's cybersecurity by applying IT security-related concepts and theories. Upon successfully passing the certification exam, which typically lasts about six hours, CISSPs can assume various job roles, including Security Manager, Security Analyst, and Chief Information Security Officer. CISSPs prioritize maintaining a robust IT security system regardless of the job title.

Certified Information Systems Security Professional Exam Format

The CISSP exam lasts for four hours and consists of multiple-choice and advanced creative questions, which will be discussed in more detail later. A score of 700 out of 1000 is required to pass the CISSP exam.

VERSAtile Reads

CISSP-Certified Information Systems Security Professional

Prior Certification		**Exam Validity**	
Not Required		3 Years	
Exam Fee		**Exam Duration**	
$599 USD		240 Minutes	
No. of Questions		**Passing Marks**	
125-175 Questions		700 out of 1000	

Recommended Experience

Minimum of five years of work experience in the domains of the CISSP CBK. Additional credential from the (ISC)² approved list. Education credit will only satisfy one year of experience.

Exam Format

Multiple Choice and advanced innovative items

Languages

English

How Much Do CISSP Holders Earn?

CISSPs are relatively rare in the industry, so those who pass the certification exam and meet the requirements are typically well-paid.

According to various sources, the average salary for a CISSP certified professional can vary depending on factors such as experience, location, and specific job title. Here's a breakdown from a few reputable sources:

- ZipRecruiter: Reports an average annual salary of $112,302 in the United States (as of March 15, 2024). They also provide a salary range from $21,000 to $165,000, with the 25th percentile at $95,500 and the 75th percentile at $128,000.
- Destination Certification: Offers average salary ranges based on job titles. For example, Chief Information Security Officers (CISOs) with CISSP certification can earn an average of $173,726, while Information Security Analysts might earn an average of $76,979.
- Simplilearn: States an average annual salary of $116,573 globally, indicating that CISSP certification is among the top-paying IT certifications.

Overall, CISSP certification can significantly boost your earning potential in the cybersecurity field. While exact salaries vary based on factors like experience and location, CISSPs can expect to earn anywhere from $75,000 to over $170,000 annually.

On the contrary, according to the Certification Magazine-Salary Survey 75 report, average salaries are as follows:

Region	Average Salary (in U.S. Dollars)
Globally	$123,490
United States	$135,510

The average global salaries reported by (ISC)² and CertMag differ due to variations in methodology. CertMag's figures encompass both U.S. and non-U.S. salaries, while (ISC)²'s statistics are derived from a broader industry-wide study, potentially offering a more representative view of actual averages. CertMag's data is based on a smaller sample size of only 55 respondents, whereas (ISC)²'s data likely involves a larger and more diverse sample.

What Experience is Required to Become a CISSP?

Despite the growing demand for CISSPs, (ISC)² imposes stringent qualifications to ensure that only highly capable and experienced professionals earn the title. While the industry offers lucrative opportunities, the requirements for CISSPs are comprehensive.

Firstly, CISSP applicants must possess at least five years of relevant working experience in IT security. This experience must align with the eight domains of the (ISC)² CISSP CBK:

1. Security and Risk Management
2. Asset Security
3. Security Architecture and Engineering
4. Communication and Network Security
5. Identity and Access Management (IAM)
6. Security Assessment and Testing
7. Security Operations
8. Software Development Security

Moreover, to meet the requirements of these domains, the (ISC)² mandates experience in any of the following positions:

- Chief Information Security Officer
- Chief Information Officer
- Director of Security
- IT Director/Manager
- Security Systems Engineer
- Security Analyst
- Security Manager
- Security Auditor
- Security Architect
- Security Consultant
- Network Architect

VERSAtile Reads

Job Opportunities with CISSP Certifications

Roles of CISSP-Certified Professionals:

Information Security Analyst

In the role of an Information Security Analyst, individuals with CISSP certification play a critical role in strengthening an organization's digital infrastructure and systems. They are responsible for analyzing and implementing robust security measures to proactively defend against a wide range of cyber threats, ensuring the resilience of the organization's information assets.

Security Consultant

CISSP-certified professionals serve as adept Security Consultants, offering specialized guidance in crafting and implementing security protocols. Their role involves meticulous examination of existing security frameworks, providing strategic insights, and implementing tailored solutions to fortify against evolving cyber threats and vulnerabilities. They assess clients' specific security needs, ensuring robust protection against potential risks.

Chief Information Security Officer (CISO)

As Chief Information Security Officers, CISSP-certified experts lead and manage an organization's comprehensive security program. They formulate and execute strategies to safeguard information assets, ensuring the highest standards of cybersecurity.

Security Software Developer

CISSP professionals in this role focus on developing secure software and applications. Their expertise ensures that the software development process integrates robust security measures, protecting against vulnerabilities and potential breaches.

Risk Manager

CISSP-certified Risk Managers identify and mitigate potential security risks within an organization. They conduct thorough risk assessments, develop mitigation strategies, and implement measures to minimize the impact of security threats.

These roles highlight the versatility and importance of CISSP certification across various domains. They underscore the crucial role CISSP professionals play in maintaining a secure and resilient digital landscape.

Benefits of CISSP Certification

- Demonstrates working knowledge of information security.
- Provides a career differentiator, enhancing credibility and marketability.
- Grants access to valuable resources such as peer networking and idea exchange.
- Offers access to a network of global industry experts and subject matter/domain experts.
- Facilitates access to broad-based security information resources.
- Provides a business and technology orientation to risk management.

Alternative Paths to Achieving CISSP Certification

Not everyone meets the strict CISSP certification requirements. However, there are alternative paths to enter the industry:

1. **Become an (ISC)² Associate:** By working as an (ISC)² Associate, individuals can fast-track their cybersecurity career despite lacking the requisite experience. This role provides opportunities for learning and growth within the industry.

2. **Obtain CompTIA Certifications:** CompTIA certifications, such as A+, Security+, and Network+, can help kickstart a cybersecurity career by bolstering credentials and demonstrating specific skills and knowledge.

3. **Pursue SSCP Certification:** Another option for meeting CISSP requirements is to earn the Systems Security Certified Professional (SSCP) credential from (ISC)². This certification serves as a stepping stone toward CISSP certification while providing comprehensive preparation and understanding of the field.

Demand of CISSP Certification in 2024

The demand for CISSP certification is expected to remain strong in 2024 for several reasons:

- **Growing Cybersecurity Threats:** As cybercrime continues to rise, organizations are increasingly looking for qualified professionals to protect their data and systems. The CISSP certification validates a candidate's understanding of cybersecurity best practices and makes them more competitive in the job market.
- **Global Recognition:** CISSP is a vendor-neutral certification that is recognized worldwide. This makes it a valuable asset for professionals who want to work in any industry or location.
- **Focus on Security Management:** CISSP goes beyond technical skills and emphasizes security management principles. This makes CISSP holders well-suited for leadership roles in cybersecurity.

Chapter 02: Security and Risk Management

Introduction

Organizations, driven by their primary goals of profitability or service provision, often find security practices burdensome. The evolving threat landscape requires businesses to deploy and maintain various security measures, navigate complex regulatory frameworks, and adapt to emerging security laws and standards. In this challenging environment, attackers target customer data, company secrets, and funds through identity theft, economic espionage, and complex digital methods. Organizations must embrace a holistic approach to security, covering technologies, procedures, and processes to safeguard market share, customers, and finances.

This chapter outlines the necessary disciplines for organizations to implement security comprehensively. It emphasizes the importance of developing an enterprise-wide security program encompassing technologies and processes. Security professionals need to understand a wide range of technologies, methodologies, and processes to identify and improve deficiencies in existing security programs.

The chapter starts with basic security ideas and gets more complex. It highlights understanding security and risks well, including accidental and environmental ones. Planning for business emergencies is vital. It ends with talks about people, rules, and doing the right thing in security.

Fundamental Principles of Security

- **Core goals:** Availability, Integrity, and Confidentiality (AIC or CIA triad).
- Security controls are designed to protect these core goals against risks, threats, and vulnerabilities.

Availability
- Ensures reliable and timely access to resources for authorized users.
- Requires protection against both internal and external threats affecting business processes.
- Operational environment should be understood to mitigate availability weaknesses.

Integrity
- Maintains accuracy and reliability of information and systems.
- Prevents unauthorized modification of data.
- Integrity threats include viruses, logic bombs, back doors, and user mistakes.
- Protection measures include strict access controls, intrusion detection, and hashing.

Confidentiality
- Maintains necessary discretion during data processing and transmission.
- Protects against unauthorized disclosure and includes defense against social engineering.
- Encrypted data storage and transmission, access control, and data classification enhance confidentiality.

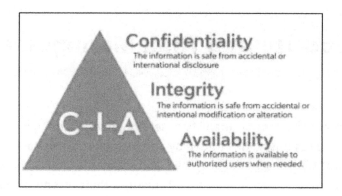

Balanced Security

- Often, security focuses mainly on confidentiality, while integrity and availability may be neglected.
- The integrity and availability threats can be overlooked and only dealt with after they are properly compromised.
- Different assets may require varying levels of protection based on the AIC triad.

.

Balanced Security Controls and Their AIC Components

- Implementing controls to meet AIC requirements is more complex than it seems.
  - **Availability:** RAID, clustering, load balancing, backups, co-location, failover configurations.
  - **Integrity:** Hashing, configuration management, change control, access control, digital signing, Transmission cyclic redundancy check (CRC) functions.
  - **Confidentiality:** Data encryption (at rest and in transit), access control.

Security Definitions

- A vulnerability is a weakness in a system that can be exploited, such as software bugs, hardware flaws, or procedural gaps.
- A threat is a potential danger that exploits a vulnerability, while a threat agent is the entity that actually exploits the vulnerability.
- Risk is the probability of a threat exploiting a vulnerability and the impact it would have on the business.
- An exposure is when an organization is open to potential losses due to vulnerabilities.
- Controls or countermeasures are action taken to mitigate risks, such as firewalls, password management, and security training.
- **Importance of Understanding Terms:**
  These terms are critical to grasp as they form the core concepts of security.
  Confusing these terms can lead to miscommunication and ineffective security measures.
  It's essential for security teams to have a common language to avoid confusion and ensure proper enforcement of security protocols.
- **Examples of Concepts:**
  Unpatched software is a vulnerability that can lead to malware attacks (threats).
  The risk is how likely it is for the malware to cause damage and the extent of that potential damage.
  If a company's environment is infiltrated by a virus, it means a vulnerability was exploited, resulting in exposure to loss.

Updating malware signatures and installing anti-malware software are countermeasures that reduce risk and exposure.

- **Relationships Among Terms:**
  Proper application of countermeasures can eliminate vulnerabilities and exposures, thus reducing risks. Companies can't eliminate threat agents but can protect against them by preventing the exploitation of vulnerabilities.

Control Types

- Administrative: Management-oriented like security policies, risk management, and training.
- Technical: Hardware or software like firewalls, Intrusion Detection System(IDS), encryption, and authentication mechanisms.
- Physical: Protect facilities and resources with measures like locks, security guards, and CCTV.

__Defense-in-Depth__ Layered security approach to reduce the success of attacks.
- Multilayered defenses increase the difficulty for attackers to access critical assets.
- Layers include various physical and technical controls based on asset sensitivity.

Security Layers
Defense in-Depth

1. Network Layer Security

2. Platform Layer Security

3. Application Layer Security

4. Data Layer Security

5. Response Layer Mechanism

__Control Functionalities__ Six types—preventive, detective, corrective, deterrent, recovery, and compensating.
- Preventive: Avoid incidents (e.g., policies, hiring practices, encryption).
- Detective: Identify incidents or intruders (e.g., auditing logs).
- Corrective: Fix issues after an incident (e.g., reloading computer images).
- Deterrent: Discourage potential attacks (e.g., visible CCTV).

VERSAtile Reads

- Recovery: Return to normal operations (e.g., data backup systems).
- Compensating: Alternative measures when primary control isn't feasible (e.g., fence instead of security guards).

Mapping Controls to Functionalities:
- Focus on the primary reason a control is in place when determining its functionality.
- Don't overcomplicate by considering secondary effects (consider CCTV primarily as a detective, not a deterrent).
- Use compensating controls as affordable or business-necessary alternatives to original controls.

Security Control Complexity:
- Controls can contradict or leave gaps, leading to security holes.
- All types of controls should work together harmoniously for a secure environment.

Security Through Obscurity: This is an ineffective security strategy that relies on secrecy and assumes attackers won't figure out hidden vulnerabilities, much like hiding a spare key under a doormat.

- **Proper Security Approach**: Ensuring software doesn't have flaws is better than relying on obscurity. Open-source code is not inherently less secure than proprietary compiled code.
- **Common Missteps in Security**: Examples include using in-house cryptographic algorithms instead of industry standards and changing standard port numbers, which can be easily detected.
- **Building a Security Program**: Security should be approached with a mature, structured strategy akin to building a fortress.
- **Security Program Elements**: It involves logical, administrative, and physical protection mechanisms, procedures, business processes, and people working in unison.

Security Frameworks
Various organizations have developed standards and frameworks for security management, control objectives, process management, and enterprise development.

ISO/IEC 27000 Series:
- Provides guides for organizations on managing risks to sensitive information and is a globally recognized standard.

Enterprise Architecture Development
- Organizations can follow ad hoc approaches or defined security architectures, with frameworks like Zachman, TOGAF, DoDAF, MODAF, and SABSA providing guidelines for enterprise architectures.

Security Controls Development
- Frameworks like COBIT 5, NIST SP 800-53, and COSO aim to provide business frameworks and sets of controls for IT management, US federal systems, and internal corporate controls, respectively.

Process Management Development
- Frameworks such as ITIL, Six Sigma, and CMMI offer processes for IT service management, business management strategies, and organizational development for process improvement.

Security Program Development

- Involves planning and organizing, implementing, operating, maintaining, monitoring, and evaluating. It's supported by management and involves continuous improvement.

Functionality vs. Security

- Security initiatives must balance securing an environment while allowing productivity and involve stakeholder consultation and understanding of business processes.
- Computer crime laws were established in response to the growth of technology-facilitated offenses.
- These laws typically address issues like unauthorized modification, destruction, disclosure of sensitive information, unauthorized access, and malware use.
- There is often a delay between technology adoption and the enactment of relevant laws.

Categories of Computer Crimes

- Computer-assisted crimes: Computers are used as tools to commit traditional crimes (e.g., financial theft and espionage).
- Computer-targeted crimes: Computers are the direct victims of crimes (e.g., DDoS attacks, and malware installation).
- Computer is incidental: Computers are involved but not the primary tool or target in the crime (e.g., storing illegal materials).

Examples of Computer-Assisted Crimes:

- Theft of funds from financial systems.
- Military system attacks for intelligence.
- Industrial spying and obtaining business data.
- Attacks on national infrastructure for information warfare.
- Hacktivism by attacking and defacing websites or systems.

Examples of Computer-Targeted Crimes:

- Distributed Denial-of-Service (DDoS) attacks.
- Capturing sensitive data like passwords.
- Installing destructive malware or rootkits.
- Buffer overflow attacks to gain control of systems.

Significance of Crime Categories

- Differentiating types of computer crimes helps apply existing laws to digital offenses.
- Computer-targeted crimes are unique to the digital era, whereas computer-assisted crimes could occur without computers.
- Categories help in applying traditional laws to new forms of crime involving computers.

Legislation Examples in the United States

- Various laws have been created or modified to address computer crimes (e.g., 18 USC 1029, 18 USC 1030, 18 USC 2510, 18 USC 2701, Digital Millennium Copyright Act, and Cyber Security Enhancement Act of 2002).

Complexities in Cybercrime

- Cybercrime is on the rise despite existing laws due to challenges such as identifying attackers, protecting networks, and prosecuting criminals.
- Attackers often go uncaught by using spoofed identities and cleaning logs, making tracking difficult.
- Intrusion Detection Systems (IDS) can alert companies to breaches but may not always identify the attacker.
- Attackers use compromised systems, known as zombies or bots, to form botnets for malicious activities like DDoS attacks and spam.

Electronic Assets

- Modern companies prioritize data protection, including personal, financial, and strategic information.
- Defining sensitive data and its protection is a challenge for many organizations.

The Evolution of Attacks

- Cybercriminals have shifted from hobbyist hackers to organized crime, targeting specific data for profit.
- Attackers use stealthy methods to avoid detection while stealing information for identity theft and fraud.
- Advanced Persistent Threats (APTs) are sophisticated, well-funded groups that infiltrate networks and remain undetected.
- Common Internet Crime Schemes encompass various types of cybercrimes such as auction fraud, counterfeit checks, investment fraud, and others.
- Internal threats from employees and contractors can lead to fraud and abuse due to access privileges and lack of monitoring.

International Issues

- Legal jurisdiction complications arise when cybercrimes cross international borders.
- Different countries have varying laws and cooperation levels, leading to challenges in prosecuting international cybercrime.
- Efforts like the Council of Europe Convention on Cybercrime aim to standardize international legal responses.

- **Import/Export Legal Requirements:** Organizations must comply with different countries' import and export laws, like the Wassenaar Arrangement, which controls the export of dual-use goods and technologies.

Types of Legal Systems

- **Civil (Code) Law System:** Rule-based, used in continental Europe.
- **Common Law System:** Precedent-based, developed in England.
- **Customary Law System:** Based on regional traditions and customs.
- **Religious Law System:** Based on religious texts and beliefs.
- **Mixed Law System:** Combination of different legal systems.
- **Data Protection Regulations**
  - General Data Protection Regulation (GDPR) EU regulation protecting personal data, with strict fines for non-

compliance.
- General Data Protection Regulation (GDPR) applies to any entity handling EU citizens' data, regardless of location.
- Protected data under GDPR includes names, addresses, ID numbers, and more sensitive personal information.
- Organizations must designate a Data Protection Officer (DPO) to ensure compliance.

Intellectual Property (IP) Laws

- Protect a company's or individual's creations from unauthorized use or duplication.
- Companies must take reasonable steps to safeguard their Intellectual property (IP) and demonstrate due care.
- Failure to protect IP adequately may lead to losing legal protection or cases such as wrongful termination suits.

Trade Secret

- Protects information that gives a company a competitive advantage.
- Must be confidential and actively protected through measures like Non-Disclosure Agreements (NDAs).
- No expiration as long as the information remains secret and valuable.

Copyright

- Protects the creator's right to control the use of original works.
- Lasts for the creator's life and 70 additional years.
- Issues arise with enforcement, especially with "warez" sites and international jurisdiction challenges.

Trademark

- Used to protect brand identity elements like logos, names, and colors.
- Must be actively used and registered to maintain protection.
- International trademark law is overseen by the World Intellectual Property Organization (WIPO).

Patent

- Grants exclusive rights to inventions that are novel, useful, and non-obvious.
- Usually for last 20 years from the approval date.
- Patent litigation is prevalent in technology, with companies often suing for alleged infringements.
- "Patent trolls" or Non-Practicing Entities (NPEs) acquire patents to seek licensing fees or litigation winnings without intent to produce the patented item.

Internal Protection of Intellectual Property

- Companies need to classify and protect sensitive information internally.
- Access should be controlled, audited, and employees should be informed about the confidentiality of IP resources.

Software Piracy

- Occurs when software is used or duplicated without authorization.
- Types of software licensing include freeware, shareware, commercial, academic, and bulk licenses.
- Software piracy is a global issue with significant economic damage estimated by organizations like the Bank Secrecy Act (BSA).

- Decompiling code and reverse-engineering are illegal acts that can lead to prosecution under laws like the Digital Millennium Copyright Act (DMCA).
- **Privacy Threats and Protection Approaches:** Privacy is increasingly at risk with the growth of computing technology. There are two main approaches to privacy regulation: generic (horizontal) and industry-specific (vertical) enactments. The focus is on protecting Personally Identifiable Information (PII) and balancing data collection needs against security concerns.
- **Personally Identifiable Information (PII):** PII is data that can uniquely identify an individual. It's essential to protect PII due to its use in identity theft and other crimes. Definitions of PII vary across jurisdictions and are based on risk assessments. Typical PII includes full name, national ID numbers, IP addresses, and credit card numbers.

Privacy Laws

- Privacy laws have been enacted globally in response to the need for PII protection.
- Examples include the U.S. Federal Privacy Act of 1974, The Gramm-Leach-Bliley Act, and HIPAA.
- Canada and New Zealand have enacted horizontal privacy laws, addressing privacy across all sectors.

Data Aggregation and Privacy Concerns

- Data aggregators compile and sell personal information, raising privacy risks.
- Data breaches at centralized data sources can lead to mass identity theft.

The Need for Privacy Laws

- Privacy and security are distinct concepts but often interrelated.
- Advances in data aggregation, global data flow, and technology raise the need for stronger privacy laws.
- The accessibility of data comes with dual implications, providing convenience while also harboring the potential for misuse.

Regulations in Information Security

- Regulations cover data privacy, computer misuse, software copyright, and controls on cryptography.
- Security professionals must understand laws and regulations to ensure organizational compliance.

U.S. Privacy Laws

- Federal Privacy Act of 1974: Restricts government data collection and sharing of individual records.
- Federal Information Security Management Act of 2002: Requires federal agencies to implement security programs for their information systems.
- Department of Veterans Affairs Information Security Protection Act: Enforces additional controls and reporting for the Veterans Administration (VA) after a data breach.
- Health Insurance Portability and Accountability Act (HIPAA): Sets standards for handling personal medical information.
- Health Information Technology for Economic and Clinical Health (HITECH) Act: Strengthens enforcement of HIPAA rules.
- USA PATRIOT Act: Expands law enforcement powers for surveillance and intelligence gathering.

- Gramm-Leach-Bliley Act (GLBA): Mandates financial institutions to protect customers' personal information.

Employee Privacy Issues
- Companies must address employee privacy in monitoring policies and inform employees accordingly.
- **Prescreening Personnel:** Organizations must follow legal limitations when conducting background checks on potential employees.
- **Personal Privacy Protection:** Users are encouraged to use encryption, firewalls, and antivirus software, and to shred personal documents to protect their privacy.

Data Breaches
- Data breaches are significant in cybersecurity, where unauthorized actors access protected information, causing potential harm.
- They can involve Personal Identifiable Information (PII), Intellectual Property (IP), Personal Health Information (PHI), or classified information.
- Legal and regulatory requirements are triggered by data breaches, varying widely across jurisdictions.

U.S. Laws Pertaining to Data Breaches:
- **Health Insurance Portability and Accountability Act (HIPAA):**
  - Applies to healthcare providers handling PHI.
  - Initially did not require breach notification until the HITECH Act amendment.
- **Health Information Technology for Economic and Clinical Health Act (HITECH Act):**
  - Directs Health and Human Services (HHS) to publish annual guidance on data protection controls.
  - Compliance with these controls exempts organizations from reporting breaches, while non-compliance requires reporting within 60 days.
- **Gramm-Leach-Bliley Act of 1999 (GLBA):**
  - Applies to financial and insurance institutions.
  - Mandates assessment of potential misuse of accessed customer information and notification if misuse is likely or has occurred.
- **Economic Espionage Act of 1996:**
  - Provides structure for investigating corporate espionage.
  - Protects corporate IP from unauthorized exposure or theft.
- **State Laws**
  - Most U.S. states have laws mandating disclosure of data breaches involving PII.
  - Definitions of PII and conditions for notification vary, complicating compliance.

Other Nations' Laws Pertaining to Data Breaches:
- International laws on data breach notifications are inconsistent.
- At least 12 countries have no notification requirements, posing risks of data handling outsourcing to avoid stringent laws.
- Numerous countries lack uniform data breach notification laws, leading to a patchwork of regulations worldwide.

- This legal disparity poses a risk as unscrupulous organizations may exploit jurisdictions with lax regulations by outsourcing data-handling operations to circumvent compliance challenges.

Policies, Standards, Baselines, Guidelines, and Procedures

Security programs should include policies, procedures, standards, guidelines, and baselines, with the involvement of human resources and legal departments.

Security Policy:
- Senior management or a designated body should create an overarching security policy, defining the scope and enforcement of security within the organization and addressing legal compliance.
- It should be driven by business objectives, easily understood, integrated into business processes, compliant with legislation, regularly reviewed, accessible, forward-thinking, professional, clear, and enforceable.
- Organizational policies are at the top, followed by issue-specific policies (e.g., e-mail policy), and system-specific policies for individual systems.
- Regulatory policies comply with industry regulations, advisory policies guide behavior with possible consequences, and informative policies educate on specific topics.

Standards:
- Standards are mandatory rules that ensure uniformity in technology usage and behavior within an organization.

Baselines:
- Baselines are reference points establishing a minimum level of protection, which can be used to measure future changes.

Guidelines:
- Guidelines offer recommendations for actions when no specific standard applies, providing flexibility for unforeseen circumstances.

Procedures:
- Procedures are detailed instructions for achieving goals, such as configuring systems or handling sensitive materials.

Implementation:
- To be effective, security policies and their supportive documents must be actively implemented and enforced, with employees made aware of expectations and consequences for noncompliance. This shows due care and prevents potential liability.

Risk Management
- Involves identifying and assessing risk, reducing it to an acceptable level, and maintaining that level.
- Encompasses a variety of risks, not only IT-related but also business decisions like acquisitions and product line expansions.

Holistic Risk Management
- Often misunderstood and not sufficiently prioritized by those inside and outside the security profession.
- Should be viewed as a business issue, with a focus on how risks impact the bottom line.

VERSAtile Reads

- Requires understanding of the context in which risk exists and a holistic approach across all organizational tiers.

NIST SP 800-39 Risk Management Tiers

- **Organizational Tier:** Focuses on the business as a whole, setting risk tolerance and framing the risk management approach.
- **Business Process Tier:** Deals with risks to major organizational functions and information flows.
- **Information Systems Tier:** Focuses on information system-related risks within the context of the broader organizational risk management.

Information Systems Risk Management Policy

- Needs strong commitment from senior management and a documented process aligned with the organization's mission.
- Should detail objectives, acceptable risk levels, risk identification processes, and connections to strategic planning.
- Outlines responsibilities, internal control mappings, and behavior and resource changes in response to risk analysis.

The Risk Management Team

- Varies in size and composition based on the organization's needs and resources.
- Requires:
  - A defined risk acceptance level from management.
  - Documented risk assessment and mitigation processes.
  - Security awareness training for staff.
  - Legal and regulation compliance mapping.
  - Development of metrics for risk management.
  - Integration with organizational change control processes.

The Risk Management Process (NIST SP 800-39)

- **Frame Risk:** Defines the context, assumptions, constraints, priorities, and risk tolerance.
- **Assess Risk:** Identification of threats, vulnerabilities, and potential impacts.
- **Respond to Risk:** Allocating resources to prioritize and implement controls based on the risk assessment.
- **Monitor Risk:** Ongoing monitoring to adapt to changes and ensure control effectiveness.

Threat Modeling

- Defined as describing feasible adverse effects on assets by threat sources.
- Important to focus on likely threats, not all possible ones, to optimize resource use.
- Threat modeling is used beyond risk assessment by various organizational teams.
- Considers what assets can be degraded, disrupted, or destroyed and by whom.

Vulnerabilities

- All human-made systems have vulnerabilities.
- Information systems are prone to vulnerabilities that risk confidentiality, integrity, or availability.
- Information can be compromised in three states: at rest, in motion, and in use.
- Process vulnerabilities relate to software and business processes.
- People can be vulnerable due to social engineering, social networks, and weak passwords.

Threat Modeling Methodologies

- A systematic approach is needed due to numerous potential vulnerability-threat-attack triads.
- **Attack Trees**
  - Visualize multiple paths to achieve a malicious objective.
  - Multiple conditions (leaf nodes) lead to a single goal (root node).
  - Helps to identify various ways an attacker can accomplish each objective.
- **Reduction Analysis**
  - Attack trees require significant resources; reduction analysis helps manage

  - Aims to reduce the number of attacks to consider by finding commonalities.
  - Identifies the most effective mitigation techniques by applying controls closer to the root node.
  - Controls or countermeasures are implemented to mitigate identified attacks.

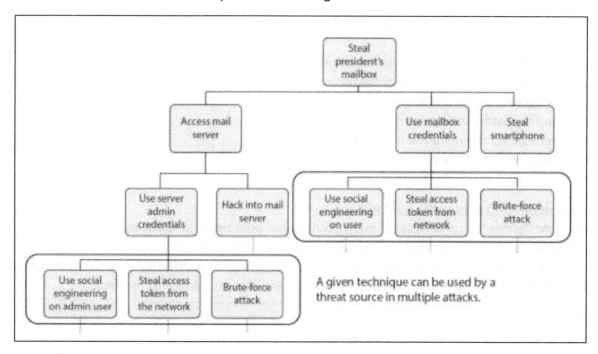

Supply Chain Risk Management

- Organizations often overlook supply chain risks, which can be exploited by attackers.
- A supply chain includes all suppliers of products and services to a company.
- Different suppliers have different security perspectives and threat models.
- Example: Target's 2013 breach via an HVAC service provider's network.

- **Supply Chain Map**

  - Essential to map out the suppliers and the flow of products and services.
  - This helps in understanding the supply chain and assessing risks.

Upstream and Downstream Suppliers

- Suppliers to your company are upstream, while your company is upstream to its customers.
- Security risks can affect both upstream and downstream elements of the supply chain.
- Companies are accountable for security issues, regardless of where they occur in the supply chain.
- Hardware Trojans can compromise security by being added at any stage of development. Counterfeit components pose risks due to lower quality and potential for embedded Trojans.
- **Software Risks**
  - Third-party software can contain Trojans, especially if custom-made.
  - Risks include reused components, malicious insiders, or interception and modification during transit.
- **Outsourcing Services Risks**
  - Outsourcing services do not outsource the associated risk of a data breach or security issue.
  - Organizations must thoroughly review service providers' security measures

Service Level Agreements (SLAs)

- SLAs are contractual guarantees of service levels with consequences for non-compliance.
- They serve as a risk mitigation tool in supply chain management by setting expectations for service provision.

Risk Management Frameworks

- Frameworks help structure the process of risk management in organizations.
- A Risk Management Framework (RMF) identifies, assesses, and manages risks to achieve an acceptable level of risk.

Categorize Information System:

- Identify systems, subsystems, and boundaries.
- Understand the system integrates with business processes, its sensitivity, and ownership.
- Determine system criticality and compliance requirements.

Select Security Controls:

- After risk assessment, establish a common baseline of controls.
- Assess new systems for specific risks and adjust controls accordingly.
- Integrate new controls into a continuous monitoring strategy.

Implement Security Controls:

- Apply the necessary controls and document changes.
- Documentation is crucial for understanding and integrating into assessment and monitoring plans.

Assess Security Controls:
- Assess the effectiveness of all security controls.
- Use independent and competent assessors.
- Document the results and update security plans with findings and recommendations.

Authorize Information System:
- Present risk and control assessments to decision-makers.
- Obtain authorization to operate the system within the architecture based on acceptable risk exposure.
- Review and adhere to a plan of action for unaddressed weaknesses.

Monitor Security Controls:
- Continuously monitor controls for effectiveness.
- Address changes in threats, vulnerabilities, and system configurations.
- Implement ongoing monitoring and continuous improvement.

Commonly Accepted Risk Management Frameworks:
- **NIST RMF (SP 800-37r1):** Used by U.S. federal agencies; focuses on the life-cycle of information systems and their certification and accreditation.
- **ISO 31000:2018:** Focuses on managing uncertainty and its effects, both negative and positive , across various aspects of an organization.
- **ISACA Risk IT:** Bridges the gap between generic frameworks and IT-centric ones; integrates well with COBIT.

Business Continuity and Disaster Recovery
- **Disaster Recovery (DR)**
    - DR focuses on minimizing the effects of a disaster and resuming operations quickly.
    - DR is IT-focused and implemented during emergency mode.

- **Business Continuity Planning (BCP)**

    - BCP deals with longer-term outages, keeping business going after a disaster.
    - BCP includes moving to alternative environments, managing communication, and maintaining operations.

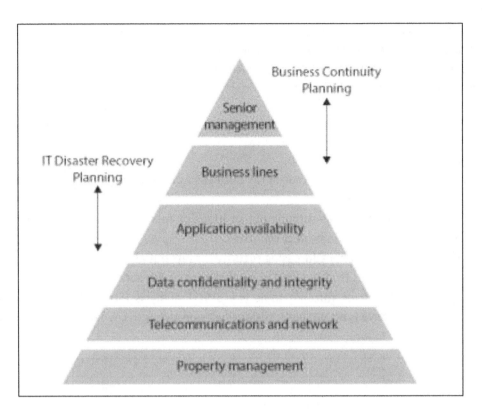

Standards and Best Practices:

- The National Institute of Standards and Technology (NIST) and ISO provide guidelines for BCP and BCM.
- Organizations should choose standards based on legal, regulatory, and operational requirements.
- NIST SP 800-34, ISO/IEC 27031, ISO 22301, and other industry guidelines offer frameworks for continuity planning.

Making BCM Part of the Enterprise Security Program

Business Continuity Management (BCM):
- BCM is the holistic process that integrates DR and BCP.
- It aims to maintain business operations under various conditions, focusing on resilience and effective response.

Key Components in BCM:
- Availability, integrity, and confidentiality must be maintained even after a disaster.
- Plans must integrate security to protect against increased vulnerability post-disaster.

Planning Considerations:
- BCP should factor in backup solutions and system redundancies.
- It's important to understand how business processes interconnect and how they can be maintained during disruptions.

Integrating BCP in the Organization:
- BCP should be part of the organization's culture and overall security program.
- A comprehensive understanding of the organization's processes is critical.
- BCP needs high-level executive support to be effective.

BCP Project Components

Project Management in BCP:

— Effective project management processes are crucial for Business Continuity Planning (BCP) and help in ensuring the efficient management of the BCP process.

— BCP projects often face challenges such as running out of funds or resources due to underestimated scopes, team members' dual responsibilities, or shifts in project priorities.

— Risk management in BCP involves not only addressing security threats but also understanding and planning for project risks, including unclear project scopes that can lead to wasted time and resources.

— Analyzing individual project objectives through tools like SWOT analysis (Strengths, Weaknesses, Opportunities, Threats) helps ensure each objective is attainable, considering team strengths, weaknesses, opportunities for success, and potential threats to project failure.

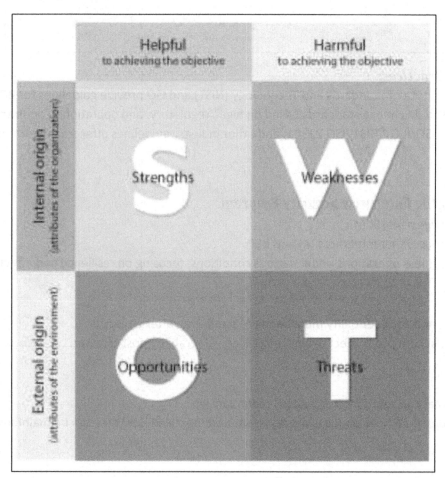

Business Impact Analysis (BIA):
- BIA identifies critical functions, resources, and the Maximum Tolerable Downtime (MTD) for each.
- It assesses the potential impact of disruptions on business functions.
- The BIA process includes interviews, data collection, risk assessment, and establishing criticality levels.

Risk Assessment in BCP:
- Risk assessment evaluates the potential impact and likelihood of threats.
- It considers both qualitative and quantitative impacts on the business.

Developing a BCP Policy:
- BCP policy provides governance and framework for BCP efforts.
- It should be reviewed and updated regularly to reflect changes in the business environment.

Management's Role in BCP:
- Management must commit to BCP, provide resources, and set policies and goals.
- They are responsible for the outcome of BCP development and must support its integration.

BCP Team's Responsibilities:
- The team must identify legal requirements, vulnerabilities, and threats.
- They should perform a BIA, outline recovery priorities, and develop resumption procedures.

Personnel Security

- People are crucial to a company's success but can also be the weakest link in security.
- Security issues often arise from personnel mistakes, lack of training, or intentional acts like fraud.
- Preventive measures can reduce risks, such as hiring qualified individuals, performing a background check, and implementing strict access controls.
- Separation of duties, split knowledge, dual control, and rotation of duties are key strategies to prevent fraud and misuse of resources.

Hiring Practices

- Hiring involves evaluating candidates' skills, character, and past behavior.
- Background checks are vital to uncovering concealed behaviors and past issues potentially harmful to the company.
- A detailed background check can reveal employment gaps, false certifications, criminal records, credit histories, and more.
- Proper hiring practices help mitigate risks, lower hiring costs, and reduce employee turnover.

Onboarding

- The onboarding process integrates new employees into the company, ensuring they understand and comply with security policies.

- New employees undergo security training, sign NDAs, and receive appropriate access credentials.

Termination
- Termination procedures are in place to prevent potential harm from disgruntled employees, including immediate account deactivation and retrieval of company property.
- Exit interviews and return of company property are encouraged but cannot be enforced without prior agreement.

Security Awareness Training
- Training is essential for changing employees' attitudes and behaviors toward security.
- Different levels of training are provided for management, staff, and technical employees.
- It's crucial to have employees acknowledge and understand the security policies and consequences of noncompliance.
- **Periodic Content Reviews**
  - Security awareness materials and curricula must be kept up to date through scheduled reviews or in response to specific events, such as policy changes or new threats.
- **Training Assessments**
  - Training effectiveness is measured by objectives and outcomes.
  - Assessments can reveal whether the training is positively affecting security posture by comparing pre-training and post-training metrics.

Degree or Certification?
- Depending on the role, a hiring manager may look for industry certifications for hands-on positions or a degree for roles requiring a holistic understanding of concepts.

Security Governance
- Security governance provides a framework for setting, communicating, and achieving security goals within an organization.
- It involves senior management expressing security goals and establishing oversight mechanisms for consistent updates on security posture.
- Even with similar security measures, differences in management involvement and integration across the organization can greatly affect the effectiveness of a company's security posture.

Metrics
- It is essential to measure the effectiveness of security programs to manage and improve them.
- Metrics provide data to assess the efficiency of security controls and financial responsibility.
- Strong management support is necessary for developing and implementing metrics.
- Policies, procedures, and standards must be established for measurement.
- Data collection methods should be repeatable, and results should be meaningful and understandable to the audience.

- **Metric and Measurement System Development**
  - International standards like ISO/IEC 27004:2016 and NIST SP 800-55, Rev 1 provide guidelines for developing security metrics.
  - Consistency in metrics is crucial for successful use and integration.
  - Metrics should match the maturity level of the security program and evolve with it.
- **Use of Metrics**
  - Metrics allow organizations to understand the health of their security program and make strategic decisions.
  - They are used in governance activities and to follow capability maturity models for incremental improvements.
  - Metrics are also applicable in process improvement models like Six Sigma and ITIL service-level targets.

Ethics

- Ethics can be subjective and are often debated, but some are widely accepted.
- **(ISC)² Code of Ethics:**
  - Protect society, public trust, and infrastructure.
  - Act honorably, honestly, justly, responsibly, and legally.
  - Provide diligent and competent service.
  - Advance and protect the profession.
- **Ethical Fallacies in Computing:**
  - Justifying hacking as skill improvement without profit motive.
  - Arguing for free and open information sharing, including confidential data.
  - Believing hacking is harmless.

Computer Ethics Institute:

- Nonprofit organization promoting ethical advancement of technology.
- Issued Ten Commandments of Computer Ethics, including not harming others, respecting privacy, and considering social consequences.

Internet Architecture Board (IAB):

- Coordinates internet design, engineering, and management.
- Issues ethics-related statements to protect internet integrity and accessibility.
- Considers acts like unauthorized access and intentional disruption to be unethical.

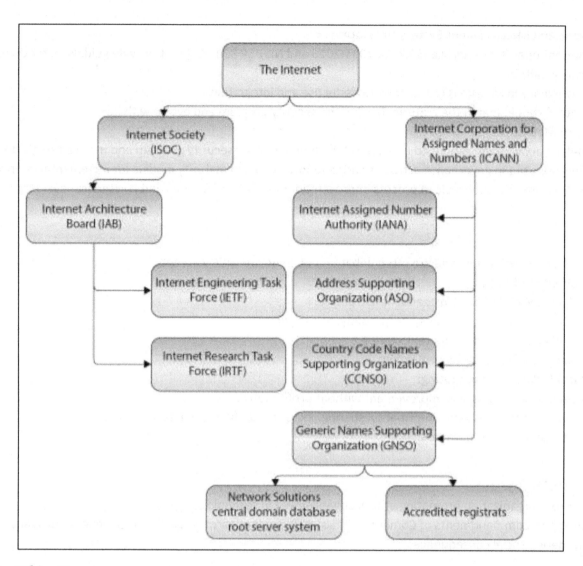

Corporate Ethics Programs:

- Regulations are prompting organizations to adopt ethical statements and programs.
- Ethical programs set a tone for top executives to act ethically and expect the same from employees.
- Ethical behavior in corporations is enforced through proper business processes and management styles.

Mind Map

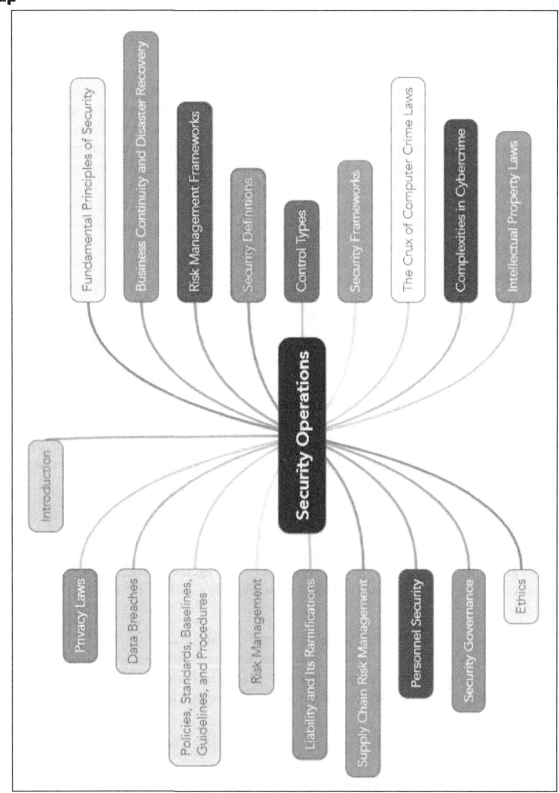

Chapter 03: Asset Security

Introduction

Assets in an organization encompass people, partners, equipment, facilities, reputation, and information, with a primary focus on protecting information assets. Information is often the most valuable asset, forming the core of every information system. This chapter, centered on the second Certified Information Systems Security Professional (CISSP) domain, emphasizes the importance of safeguarding information. Information exists within a context, created or acquired at a specific time for a particular purpose, and moves through an organization's systems, contributing value or awaiting use. The chapter introduces an information life-cycle model applicable to most organizations, addressing evaluation, use, maintenance, and proper disposal of information. It highlights organizational roles related to information assets and emphasizes the need for effective retention policies. The conclusion emphasizes identifying threats to information security and suggesting controls to prevent data loss.

Information Life-cycle

- Life-cycle models describe the changes an entity experiences during its lifetime.
- Information can generate other information, similar to reproduction.
- The life cycle of information consists of four phases: acquisition, use, archival, and disposal.

Acquisition

- Information is typically copied or created from scratch.
- Once acquired, it undergoes preparation, including the addition of metadata and indexing.
- It must be stored with policy controls, such as encryption for sensitive data and access restrictions.
- Proper planning at this stage is crucial for security and efficiency, especially in larger organizations.

Use

- Information is actively read and modified by authorized users.
- Security challenges include ensuring confidentiality, integrity, and availability.
- Consistency across data stores and compliance with policies and regulations are critical.
- Changes in information usage must align with internal policies and legal requirements.

Archival

- Information is retained for future use or due to regulatory requirements.
- Appropriate controls are necessary to prevent undetected unauthorized access or changes.
- Backups and archives serve different purposes, but both need to be protected, often through encryption.
- Risk assessments inform retention policies and ensure compliance with legal discovery, and avoid excessive costs or liabilities.

Disposal

- Data must eventually be destroyed or transferred to another party and then destroyed.
- Ensuring data is thoroughly and correctly destroyed is essential.

- Data destruction methods include wiping, degaussing, or shredding physical devices.
- Proper destruction is complex when dealing with files, database records, or systems with multiple data copies.

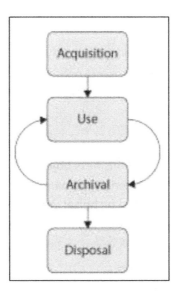

Classification

- Classification is vital for applying protective controls to information based on its value.
- Information is classified into different levels to reflect its sensitivity and criticality.
- Sensitivity relates to the potential organizational loss if information is disclosed.
- Criticality indicates the impact on business processes if information is lost.
- Classified data requires appropriate security controls based on its level.

Classification Levels

- No universal rules for classification levels; organizations decide based on their needs.
- Common commercial levels: Confidential, Private, Sensitive, and public
- Common military levels: Top Secret, Secret, Confidential, Sensitive but Unclassified and Unclassified.
- The classification scheme should fit the organization's business and security needs.
- Classifications should be clear and not overlap to avoid confusion.

Classification Controls

- Controls depend on the level of protection required.
- Includes access control, encryption, auditing, separation of duties, and periodic reviews.
- Backup and recovery, change control, physical security, information flow, and disposal actions must be defined for sensitive data.

Classification Procedure

1. Define classification levels.
2. Specify criteria for classifying data.

3. Identify data owners responsible for classification.
4. Identify data custodians responsible for maintaining security levels.
5. Indicate required security controls for each classification level.
6. Document any exceptions.
7. Provide methods for transferring data custody.
8. Review classifications periodically and communicate changes.
9. Outline procedures for declassifying data.
10. Include classification issues in security awareness training for all employees.

Layers of Responsibility

- Senior management sets the vision, goals, and business objectives.
- Functional management understands departmental roles and security impacts.
- Operational managers and staff handle detailed technical and procedural operations.
- Each layer contributes to security practices, procedures, and controls.

Senior Management Responsibility:

- Senior managers, especially in the C-suite, carry ultimate responsibility for the organization.
- They are accountable for organizational failures, fraud, and ensuring due care in information security.

Executive Management

- CEOs manage daily operations, strategic planning, and company growth but cannot delegate ultimate responsibility.
- CFOs handle accounting, financial activities, and reporting to the SEC and stakeholders.
- CIOs oversee the strategic management of information systems and technology integration.
- CPOs ensure data privacy and compliance with legal and regulatory requirements.

Data Owner

- Data owners are management members responsible for data protection and use.

Data Custodian

- Data custodians maintain and protect data following security policies.

System Owner

- System owners ensure systems have adequate security and report vulnerabilities.

Security Administrator

- Security administrators implement and maintain network security devices and software.

Supervisor
- Supervisors manage user activity and inform security changes based on employee status.

Change Control Analyst
- Change control analysts oversee the secure implementation of changes in the network or software.

Data Analyst
- Data analysts ensure data is organized and stored effectively to support business objectives.

User
- Users are responsible for following security procedures to maintain data integrity.

Auditor
- Auditors check compliance with policies, laws, and regulations, helping ensure organizational security.

Why So Many Roles?
- It is important to have a clear structure with defined roles, responsibilities, authority, communication, and enforcement capabilities.

Retention Policies
- No global consensus on data retention duration; it varies by country and sector.
- Essential to have a documented policy that's regularly audited.
- Outsourced contracts should include data retention and eradication terms.
- Using the longest legal retention time for all data can be impractical and costly.
- Different business units may have different retention needs.
- Segregate data based on specific legal retention requirements.

Developing a Retention Policy
A Retention policy should clarify the following

- **How We Retain**
  - Data must be accessible and searchable.
  - Factors to consider for data retention:

    - **Taxonomy**: Classifying data appropriately.
    - **Classification**: Securing sensitive data.
    - **Normalization**: Making data searchable with tagging schemas.
    - **Indexing**: Facilitating data searches.

  - Archiving should ideally be centralized and standardized but often requires compromise.

- **How Long We Retain**
  - Extremes of "keep nothing" or "keep everything" are not legally defensible.
  - Consult legal counsel for specific statutory, regulatory, and best practice guidance.

- **What Data We Retain**
  - Legal counsel should be involved to meet legal obligations.
  - Consider the importance of data for business and third-party relations.
  - Make deliberate and enforceable decisions about data retention.

- **e-Discovery**
  - Process of producing relevant Electronically Stored Information (ESI) for legal proceedings.
  - An adequate retention policy and procedures should make e-discovery manageable.
  - The Electronic Discovery Reference Model (EDRM) outlines steps from identification to presentation of data.

Protecting Privacy

- Privacy vs. security debate intensified after the 9/11 attacks, with a shift towards security.
- Post-Snowden leaks in 2013, the trend is swinging back towards enhanced privacy protections.
- Organizations must balance privacy and security within their information systems.

Data Owners

- Responsible for data classification and approving disclosure requests.
- Senior managers usually act as data owners.
- Policies should be in place to guide decisions on data access, with exceptions documented.

Data Processors

- Key to protecting or compromising data privacy.
- Need clear guidelines on acceptable behavior and policy adherence.
- Require training and routine auditing to ensure compliance with laws and policies.

Data Remanence

- Data deletion often leaves remnants due to how file systems operate.
- NIST SP 800-88, Rev. 1 provides guidelines to combat data remanence.

Combating Data Remanence:

- **Overwriting:** Replacing original data with random or fixed patterns.

- **Degaussing:** Wiping or reducing magnetic fields on storage media.

- **Encryption:** Storing data in encrypted form and deleting the key to render data unrecoverable.

- **Physical destruction:** Shredding or exposing media to destructive forces.

Limits on Collection

- Collect only necessary personal data for business functions.
- Privacy laws vary by country; organizations must comply with applicable regulations.

- Privacy policies should detail data collection, use, sharing, ownership, subject rights, retention, and relevant laws.

Protecting Assets

- Physical security combats theft, service interruptions, physical damage, unauthorized access, and compromised system integrity.
- Real loss includes replacement costs, productivity and reputation impact, consultant fees, and the restoration of data and production levels.
- Risk analysis involves inventory and valuation of hardware and the valuable information within.

Data Security Controls

- Controls depend on assigned value and the state of data: at rest, in motion, or in use.
- **Data at Rest**
  - Vulnerable to physical access and network threats.
  - Encrypted data is safer, but it is not always the default setting.
  - Organizations are moving towards policies requiring encryption for sensitive information, especially on portable devices.
- **Data in Motion**
  - Most vulnerable when traversing networks.
  - Strong encryption, like TLS or IPSec, is the best protection.
  - Awareness of potential man-in-the-middle attacks is crucial.
- **Data in Use**
  - Resides in primary storage and is difficult to protect as it's usually decrypted during use.
  - Side-channel attacks are a risk to data in use.
  - Secure software development practices are necessary to mitigate risks.

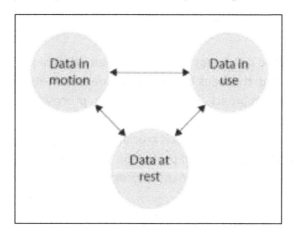

Media Controls

- Media can be electronic or non-electronic and requires diverse controls for data preservation.
- Proper environmental storage, access restrictions, and clear labeling are key practices.
- Secure disposal methods are critical to prevent data breaches.

Protecting Mobile Devices
- Mobile theft is rising with a shift from hardware to data theft.
- Protection mechanisms include inventory management, OS hardening, encryption, and remote wiping capabilities.

Paper Records
- Paper records, though less common, still require secure handling and disposal.

Safes
- Used for storing valuable items and data backups.
- Types include wall safes, floor safes, chests, depositories, and vaults.
- Safes should have periodic combination changes and include tamper detection features.

Selecting Standards
- Standards should be cost-effective and relevant to the asset's value.
- Adapting existing standards involves scoping (trimming) and tailoring (modifying) to fit specific organizational needs.

Data Leakage
- Data leaks can happen even with strong controls due to employee negligence, the most common cause.
- Costs involve remediation, notification, fines, liabilities, mitigation expenses, and direct damages.
- A company's reputation and individuals' identities may be at risk.
- **Employee Role and Awareness in Data Leakage:**
  - Employees often cause leaks due to a lack of security awareness.
  - Employers must include security in routine communications, training, and performance reviews.
  - Employees may use personal or unsecured technologies to work remotely, risking data security.

Data Leak Prevention (DLP):
- Focused on preventing sensitive data access by unauthorized external parties.
- Not all data is equally protected; the focus is on data considered sensitive and valuable.
- DLP should be part of a holistic approach, integrating people, processes, and information.
- **General Approaches to DLP:**
  - Integration with risk management processes is crucial.
  - Understanding data inventories, flows, and protection strategies is key.
  - Technology alone is insufficient; a comprehensive program encompassing policies and culture is necessary.
- **Data Inventories:**
  - Identify and characterize all sensitive data within the organization.
  - Prioritize data based on importance, format, and media.
  - Understand the value and risks associated with less critical but sensitive data.
- **Data Flows:**
  - Data must move according to business processes, requiring an understanding of data flows for DLP.
  - DLP sensors should be placed not just at network perimeters but also internally, based on data flows.

- **Data Protection Strategy:**
  - Must consider the risk of adversaries gaining internal network access.
  - Strategies include backup and recovery, data life-cycle, physical security, security culture, privacy, and organizational change.
- **Implementation, Testing, and Tuning of DLP:**
  - Select DLP solutions based on an organization's specific requirements.
  - Testing should verify that authorized processes work and that unauthorized processes are prevented.
  - Continual maintenance and improvement are necessary.
- **Network DLP (NDLP):**
  - Applies data protection policies to data in motion, typically at network perimeters.
  - NDLP devices may not detect leaks on unprotected subnetworks or off-premises.
- **Endpoint DLP (EDLP):**
  - Applies policies to data at rest and in use on each endpoint device.
  - Offers protection at the point of data creation and while data is in use.
  - Complexity and cost are higher, with unique challenges for each endpoint.
- **Hybrid DLP:**
  - Combines NDLP and EDLP for comprehensive coverage.
  - Most expensive and complex but offers the best protection across an enterprise.

Mind Map

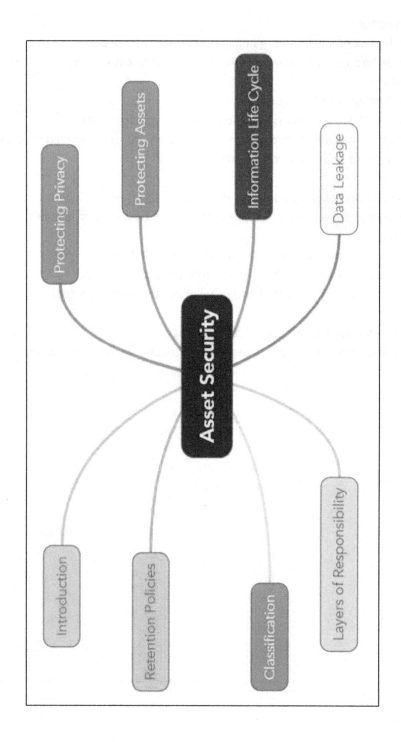

Chapter 04: Security Architecture and Engineering

Introduction

Organizations face various security concerns, such as safeguarding confidential database data, securing internet-connected web farms, ensuring data integrity in business applications, defending against external attackers, managing malware threats, maintaining internal data consistency, and addressing mobile device security. These issues not only impact productivity and profitability but also entail legal and liability risks.

Companies must prioritize security measures during product development or acquisition to avoid accountability for security breaches. Security is most effective when designed into the foundation of a product rather than added as an afterthought. Integration involves engineering, implementation, testing, evaluation, and potential certification and accreditation. Assessing a product's security requires evaluating its claims of availability, integrity, and confidentiality.

However, purchasers often lack the necessary understanding to ask pertinent questions about cryptographic key protection, encryption algorithms, software development life cycle models, hashing algorithms, message authentication codes, fault tolerance, and redundancy options. This chapter delves into security architecture and engineering, covering evaluations and ratings by governments and agencies. A significant focus is on cryptology, a fundamental aspect of security controls. The chapter also addresses physical security measures to prevent unauthorized access. Before exploring these concepts, it provides an understanding of system-based architectures and their components.

System Architecture

- Architecture helps understand complex systems through various views.
- It is a high-level conceptual tool that outlines structure, behavior, components, and relationships within a system
- Architects should focus on secure system architecture to prevent inherent system insecurities.
- **Architecture vs. Design vs. Development:**
    - Architecture: Describes major components and their interactions and answers high-level questions about system usage, environment, security, and communication.
    - Development: Refers to the system's entire lifecycle, including planning, building, testing, deployment, maintenance, and retirement.
    - Design: Detailed phase within development, following the architecture phase, outlining everything needed to build the system.
- **Understanding System:**
    - The term "system" can refer to an individual computer, application, subsystems, networks, or complex enterprise environments.
    - The scope of the system must be understood before development or evaluation.
- **Standards for System Architectures:**
    - IEEE Standard 1471 evolved into ISO/IEC/IEEE 42010, aiming to standardize system architecture practices.
    - The standard aims to improve the quality, interoperability, extensibility, portability, and security of systems.
- **Key Terms Defined in ISO/IEC/IEEE 42010:2011:**
    - Architecture: Fundamental organization of a system.
    - Architecture Description (AD): Formal collection of documents conveying architecture.

- Stakeholder: Any individual or organization with interest in the system.
- View: System representation from the perspective of a set of concerns.
- Viewpoint: Conventions for constructing and using a view.
- **Stakeholders and Views:**
  - Different stakeholders such as users, operators, maintainers, developers, and suppliers have unique concerns (performance, functionality, security, etc.).
  - Architecture must address each stakeholder's concerns through specific views.
  - Views adhere to viewpoints and provide relevant information to stakeholders.
- **Security in System Architecture:**
  - Security is a growing concern that needs to be integrated from the architecture phase.
  - Systems should be designed with security "baked in" rather than "bolted on" during development.

Computer Architecture

- Includes CPU, memory, logic circuits, storage, input/output devices, security components, buses, and networking interfaces.
- Complexity in architecture leads to vulnerabilities and countermeasures for security.

The Central Processing Unit (CPU)

- Acts as the computer's brain, executing instructions from memory.
- Different CPUs have unique architectures and instruction sets, requiring compatible operating systems.
- Contains millions of transistors, performing operations with electrical signals representing binary code.
- Utilizes registers for storing instruction locations and status information.
- The Arithmetic Logic Unit (ALU) within the CPU performs mathematical and logical operations.
- **Operating System and Applications**
  - Comprised of instructions that manipulate data.
  - Instructions and data are passed to the CPU for processing.
  - Applications rely on the CPU and system components to function.
- **Control Unit**
  - Manages and synchronizes system operations, akin to a traffic cop.
  - Determines priority and execution timing of application instructions.
  - CPU time is divided into slices, creating an illusion of multitasking.

Multiprocessing

- Modern computers may have multiple CPUs.
- Operating systems must be designed for multi-CPU use.
- Symmetric mode distributes tasks as needed, while asymmetric mode dedicates CPUs to specific tasks or applications.

Memory Types

- **Random Access Memory (RAM)**
  - Temporary, volatile storage.
  - Used for read/write activities by the OS and applications.

- **Read-Only Memory (ROM)**
  - Nonvolatile, data is retained when power is off.
  - ROM, PROM, EPROM, EEPROM, and Flash memory types exist, each with different characteristics.
- **Cache Memory**
  - High-speed memory for frequently accessed data.
- **Memory Management and Protection**
  - Memory is controlled to prevent corruption and unauthorized access.
  - Techniques like memory mapping, Address Space Layout randomization (ASLR), and Data Execution Prevention (DEP) are used for protection.
- **Buffer Overflow**
  - Occurs when too much data is input into a process, potentially leading to the execution of malicious code.
  - Attackers need to know buffer sizes and memory addresses to exploit vulnerabilities.
- **Memory Protection Techniques**
  - ASLR randomizes memory address spaces to obscure targets from attackers.
  - DEP marks certain memory locations as non-executable to reduce risk.
- **Memory Leaks**
  - Poorly written code might fail to release memory, leading to system performance issues.
  - Garbage collectors are used to reclaim unused memory.

Operating Systems (OS)

- Provide environments for applications and users.
- Manage processes, memory, I/O, and CPU.
- Offer multiprogramming, allowing multiple applications to load into memory.

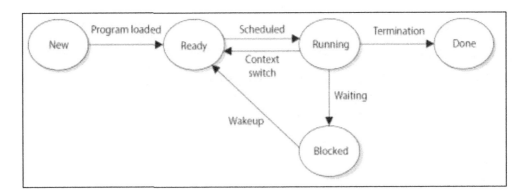

Process Management:

- Converts static code into dynamic processes when loaded into memory.
- Assigns resources like memory segments and CPU time slots.
- Supports multitasking, enabling simultaneous processing of applications.
- Has evolved from cooperative to preemptive multitasking.
- **Process Models**:
  - System like Unix and Linux allow processes to spawn child processes.
  - Processes can be in running, ready, or blocked states.
  - Operating systems manage a process table with status information.

- **Thread Management**:
  - Processes generate threads for CPU processing.
  - Threads contain instruction sets and data.
  - Multithreaded applications can run multiple threads simultaneously.
- **Process Scheduling**:
  - Operating systems schedule and synchronize process activities.
  - Use algorithms to manage the time-sharing of the CPU.
- **Process Activity**:
  - Processes share resources and require isolation for stability.
  - Operating systems ensure processes do not corrupt shared memory or data.

Memory Management

- Critical for system stability and security.
- Goals include abstraction for programmers and protecting OS and applications.
- Memory manager five basic responsibilities are relocation, protection, sharing, logical and physical organization.
- Virtual Memory:
  - Combines RAM and secondary storage.
  - Swap space on the hard drive extends RAM capabilities.
  - Virtual memory paging manages data between the hard drive and RAM.

Input/Output Device Management:

- Manages and controls I/O devices.
- Uses device drivers to communicate with device controllers.

CPU Architecture Integration

- Operating systems and CPUs need compatible architectures.
- CPUs operate based on instruction sets.
- Operating systems use ringed architectures for security.

Operating System Architectures:

- Monolithic: All OS processes run in kernel mode.
- Layered: Hierarchical layers of OS functionality.
- Microkernel: Core OS processes in kernel mode; others in user mode.
- Hybrid Microkernel: Core processes in microkernel and others in a client/server model.

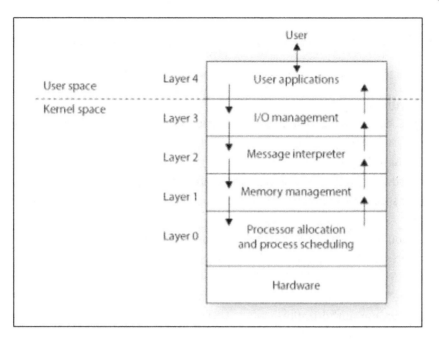

Virtual Machine:

- Allows multiple OS environments on a single hardware.
- Managed by a hypervisor that controls guest OS instances.
- Provides benefits like cost savings, security, and system consolidation.

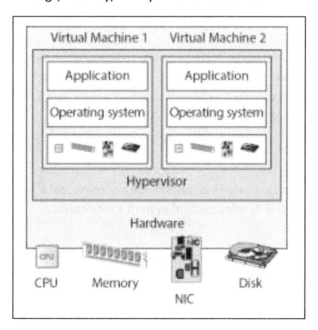

System Security Architecture

- System architecture is viewed from a security perspective, focusing on core components for computing systems.
- Goals for system security are defined specifically to guide the development of a secure system.

Security Policy
- A security policy is a high-level directive that outlines the foundational goals for system security.

- Goals must be specific to establish a desired end state and plan to achieve them.

Security Architecture Requirements:
- In the 1970s, the U.S. government defined security requirements for computer systems, resulting in the Trusted Computer System Evaluation Criteria.
- **Trusted Computing Base (TCB):**
  - TCB includes all hardware, software, and firmware components that enforce system security policy.
  - It is responsible for supporting and enforcing security policy and avoiding unauthorized system behavior.
- **Security Perimeter**
  - It is an imaginary boundary separating trusted components within the TCB from untrusted ones.
  - Communication between components inside and outside the TCB is controlled through strict interfaces.
- **Reference Monitor**
  - An abstract machine that mediates all access between subjects (users, processes) and objects (files, resources), ensuring proper authorization.
  - Centralized tamperproof component within the operating system's kernel.
- **Security Kernel**
  - Implements and enforces the reference monitor concept.
  - It is tamperproof and must be concise enough to be thoroughly tested and verified.
- **System Trust**
  - Trust in a system is determined by its adherence to the security policy and the effectiveness of its security mechanisms.
  - Systems are evaluated and rated based on their ability to enforce the security policy.
- **Security Policy Implementation:**
  - Operating systems implement various mechanisms such as access rights, permissions, and memory protection to meet the abstract concepts of security policies.

Security Models

Security models translate security policy goals into system terms using data structures and techniques. They are represented mathematically and guide the development of system specifications.

Bell-LaPadula Model
- Focuses on confidentiality in multilevel security systems.
- Contains three rules:
  - Simple security rule: No read-up
  - Star Property rule: No write-down (cannot write to lower security level).
  - Strong star property rule: Read and write at the same security level.

Biba Model:
- Addresses data integrity, not confidentiality.
- Contains three rules:
  - Integrity axiom: No write-up

- o Simple integrity axiom: No read-down (cannot read from lower integrity level).
- o Invocation property: Cannot invoke higher integrity level services.

Clark-Wilson Model:
- Focuses on integrity through well-formed transactions and separation of duties.
- Elements include users, Transformation Procedures (TPs), Constrained Data Items (CDIs), Unconstrained Data Items (UDIs), and Integrity Verification Procedures (IVPs).
- Access triple concept: Users modify CDIs only through TPs.

Non-interference Model:
- Ensures actions at a higher security level don't affect lower-level actions.
- Prevents information leakage through state changes.
- Addresses covert channels.

Covert Channels:
- Two types: storage and timing
  Storage covert channels involve the unauthorized use of storage resources to hide information, while timing covert channels exploit variations in timing or delays to convey hidden data clandestinely.
- Allow unauthorized communication between processes.

Brewer and Nash Model (Chinese Wall):
- Protects against conflicts of interest.
- Access controls change dynamically based on the user's actions.

Graham-Denning Model:
- Defines eight primitive protection rights for securely managing objects and subjects.

Harrison-Ruzzo-Ullman Model:
- Focuses on access rights integrity.
- Ensures that subjects perform only a finite set of operations on objects.

Systems Evaluation
- Focuses on evaluating security-relevant parts of a system: TCB, access control, reference monitor, kernel, and protection mechanisms.
- Determines the relationship and interaction between components to assess protection levels.

Common Criteria
- Initiated in 1993 by international collaboration for global security standards.
- Codified as ISO/IEC 15408, currently at version 3.1.
- Simplifies the evaluation process and standardizes assurance levels internationally.

- **Evaluation Assurance Levels (EALs)**
  - Range from EAL1 (functionally tested) to EAL7 (formally verified design and tested).

- Higher EALs indicate more detailed and thorough testing and verification.

- **Protection Profiles**
    - Describe the security requirements and the necessary EAL for a product.
    - Include environmental assumptions, objectives, and the strength of protection mechanisms.
    - Help consumers identify security needs; developers and evaluators use them to ensure product compliance.

- **Components of the Common Criteria**
    - Protection Profile (PP): Describes the needed security solution.
    - Target of Evaluation (TOE): Product proposed to provide the security solution.
    - Security Target: Vendor's explanation of product's security functionality and mechanisms.
    - Security Functional Requirements: Specific security functions required.
    - Security Assurance Requirements: Measures for development and evaluation compliance.
    - Packages/EALs: Bundled requirements to achieve specific EAL ratings.

- **SO/IEC 15408 Standard**
    - Consists of three main parts: Introduction/general model, security functional components, and security assurance components.
    - Defines terms, TOE concept, evaluation context, and PP and security target guidelines.

Why Put a Product Through Evaluation?
- Offers a competitive advantage to vendors and meets government purchasing requirements.
- Ensures unbiased, independent third-party testing and evaluation.
- Process is costly and time-consuming, often pursued if assurance ratings influence purchasing decisions.
- In the U.S., DoD is a significant buyer influencing vendors to undergo the Carbon copy (CC) evaluation process.

Certification vs. Accreditation
- Certification is a technical evaluation of security components and compliance to ensure a system or product is appropriate for a specific use.
- Accreditation is the management's formal acceptance of a system's security and functionality after reviewing certification information.

Certification
- Involves a detailed assessment using evaluation, risk analysis, verification, testing, and auditing.
- Aims to ensure a product or system fits a customer's specific needs, providing the necessary functionality and security.

Accreditation
- Management reviews certification findings and decides whether to accept a system and any necessary corrective actions.
- Represents an understanding of the system's protection level and associated security risks.

Continuous Process
- Certification and accreditation should be ongoing due to software, systems, and environments changes.

- New certifications and accreditations should occur with any major system changes or environmental modifications.
- **Accountability in Accreditation**
  - Management is held accountable for the risks when signing off on new products.
  - There's a shift from perfunctory approvals ("pencil whipping") to more serious consideration due to increased responsibility and regulations.
- **Certification and accreditation in the Context of FISMA**
  - FISMA (Federal Information Security Management Act of 2002) requires federal agencies to ensure and report on the security of their information systems.
  - Certification and accreditation are core components of FISMA compliance.
  - There's a move from periodic certification and accreditation (C&A) processes to continuous monitoring to meet these requirements.

Open vs. Closed Systems

Open Systems

- Built on standards, protocols, and interfaces with published specifications
- Provide interoperability among products from different vendors.
- Allow for easy communication and integration between systems.
- Support add-ons and enhancements from third parties.
- Most current systems are open, facilitating cross-platform communication (e.g., Windows, macOS, Unix).

Closed Systems

- Do not follow industry standards for architecture.
- Lack of interoperability and standard interfaces hinders seamless communication among diverse systems and add-on features.
- Proprietary nature limits communication to similar systems.
- Potentially more secure due to less common understanding and fewer tools to exploit them.
- Security through obscurity is not reliable; systems should be built and maintained with security in mind.
- Less common due to the benefits of open architectures.

Systems Security

- Systems often rely on other systems, creating interdependent vulnerabilities.
- Different system classifications help address and mitigate vulnerabilities.

Client-Based Systems

- Operate entirely on one device, with potential weak authentication and data often stored in plaintext.

Client/Server Systems

- Require interactions across a network, with varying tiers in architecture.
- Web browsers connecting to web servers are common examples.

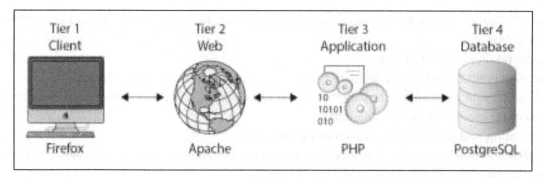

Distributed Systems
- Multiple computers work together across a network.
- Security is complex due to the number of devices involved.

Cloud Computing
- Offers efficiencies and scalability with various service models: SaaS, PaaS, and IaaS.
- Security depends on user policies and service provider contracts.

Parallel Computing
- Utilizes multiple CPUs or computers to divide tasks for efficiency.
- Can operate at bit-level, instruction-level, task-level, and data parallelism.

Database Systems
- Main issues include aggregation (combining restricted data from different sources) and inference (deducing sensitive information).
- Security measures include content- and context-dependent access control.

Web-Based Systems
- Websites are primary targets, requiring adherence to security principles.
- Emphasize input sanitation, encryption, and secure failure.

Mobile Systems
- Mobile devices are increasingly used but often lack robust security measures.
- Corporate mobile security policies should manage devices centrally and enforce security features.

Cyber-Physical Systems
- Integration of computers with physical devices to perform tasks.
- Includes embedded systems like traffic lights and the Internet of Things (IoT).

A Few Threats to Review
- **Embedded Systems**
  - Inexpensive, compact systems controlling devices, vulnerable due to invisibility and network connectivity.

- **Internet of Things (IoT)**
  - Network of connected devices, posing challenges for authentication, encryption, and updates.

- **Industrial Control Systems (ICS)**
  - Designed to control physical devices in industrial processes.
  - Different types include PLCs, DCS, and SCADA systems, each with unique purposes and security considerations.

- **Programmable Logic Controllers (PLC)**
  - Control electromechanical processes, with a trend towards standardization and network-enablement.

- **Distributed Control Systems (DCS)**
  - Network of control devices for local industrial processes, moving towards standard protocols.

- **Supervisory Control and Data Acquisition (SCADA)**
  - Controls large-scale physical processes over distances, often using dedicated communication links.

- **ICS Security**
  - Vulnerability increases with network connectivity.
  - Recommendations include risk management, network segmentation, applying least privilege, and patch management.

- **Software Vulnerabilities and Bugs:**
  - Complex functionality in software often leads to vulnerabilities.
  - Attackers exploit system operations and functionality, creating a constant battle with security professionals.
  - An estimated average of six defects per 1,000 lines of code exists, leading to potential millions of bugs in large codebases like Google's.

Maintenance Hooks

- Maintenance hooks are back doors within software for developer use.
  - They provide developers with direct code access, bypassing regular controls.
  - Initially helpful for development, if not removed, they pose significant security risks.
  - Attackers can exploit these hooks for malicious actions.
  - Despite security advancements, maintenance hooks are still used and can be present in older software.

Time-of-Check/Time-of-Use Attacks

- **Countermeasures:**
  - Programmers are responsible for removing maintenance hooks before software goes into production.
  - Code reviews, unit tests, and quality assurance should check for any back doors.
  - Users have limited measures to prevent maintenance hooks, but vendors often release patches to address these vulnerabilities.
  - Preventive measures include host-based intrusion detection systems, file system encryption, and auditing to detect back door usage.

Cryptography in Context

- Cryptography is key to protecting system architectures by encoding data so only intended recipients can read it.
- It aims to make unauthorized access to encrypted information too costly or time-consuming.

The History of Cryptography

- Originated around 2000 BC in Egypt with hieroglyphics, which evolved from ceremonial use to practical encryption.
- The Hebrew Atbash method involved a simple alphabet substitution cipher.
- Spartans used a scytale cipher, dependent on a staff's size, to encrypt messages.
- Julius Caesar developed a cipher by shifting alphabet letters by three positions.
- ROT13 was used in the 1980s in online forums to hide inappropriate material by shifting letters 13 spaces.
- Blaise de Vigenère created a polyalphabetic cipher in the 16th century, increasing encryption complexity.
- Cryptography was refined through the Middle Ages and became common in military communication by the late 1800s.
- The Enigma machine in WWII represented a significant advancement but was eventually broken by allied cryptographers.
- **Evolution and Importance of Cryptography**
  - Mary, Queen of Scots, and Benedict Arnold's historical use of cryptography highlights its importance in security and espionage.
  - William Frederick Friedman is considered the "Father of Modern Cryptography."
  - Computers expanded the possibilities for encryption, leading to the development of complex algorithms like IBM's Lucifer project.
  - DES, developed in 1976, was a standard for encryption but was superseded by more secure systems like Triple DES.
  - Cryptography is now embedded in various technologies to protect data across many platforms.
- **Cryptanalysis and Cryptology**
  - Cryptanalysis is the study of breaking encryption and reverse-engineering algorithms.
  - It's used by both security professionals to improve systems and by hackers to gain unauthorized access.
  - Cryptology encompasses both cryptanalysis and cryptography.
- **Current Role of Cryptography**
  - Cryptography is deeply integrated into communications and computing, essential for military, government, and private business functions.
  - Dependence on technology correlates with dependence on cryptography for maintaining secrets.

Cryptography Definitions and Concepts

- **Encryption:** transforms readable data (plaintext) into unreadable data (ciphertext).
  - Plaintext can be a document for humans or executable code for computers.
  - Ciphertext is unreadable without decryption, securing data transmission over insecure channels.
- **Cryptosystems:** provide encryption and decryption through hardware or software.
- **Encryption Algorithm:** dictates the encryption process and is often a complex mathematical formula.
- **Keys** are secret values essential for encrypting and decrypting data.
- **Key Analogy**: Like individual keys for the same brand of locks, encryption keys are unique per lock (cryptosystem).

- **Keyspace**: The range of values from which a key can be generated; larger keyspace means more secure keys.
- **Key Sizes**: Commonly 128, 256, 512, or 1,024 bits, with larger sizes, providing more potential combinations and security.
- **Overhear**: Capturing an encrypted message is useless without the key, even if the algorithm is known.
- **Cryptosystem Components**: Software, protocols, algorithms, and keys. (e.g., Pretty Good Privacy - PGP)

Kerckhoffs' Principle
- Advocates for public knowledge of cryptography algorithms, with the key being the only secret.
- Supports the notion that public scrutiny of the algorithm can lead to stronger security.
- Contrasts with government practices, where algorithms are kept secret.

The Strength of the Cryptosystem
- Defined by the algorithm, key secrecy and size, initialization vectors, and their interplay.
- Encryption strength refers to the difficulty in deciphering the algorithm or discovering the key.
- Brute-force attacks try all possible keys, and their feasibility depends on computational power.
- Cryptography strength is also known as work factor, the estimated effort to break the system.
- The level of encryption should match the sensitivity of the data.
- Key protection is crucial; sharing keys can significantly weaken encryption.

One-Time Pad
- Considered a perfect and unbreakable encryption scheme if used correctly.
- Invented in 1917 by Gilbert Vernam, also known as the Vernam cipher.
- Uses random values in a pad and XOR (exclusive-OR) for encryption and decryption.
- Unbreakable when the pad is truly random, used once, and is as long as the message.
- Distribution and protection of the pad are challenging, making it impractical for many situations.
- Still used by militaries as a backup encryption method.
- **Requirements**
  - The pad must contain truly random values.
  - Each pad can only be used once.
  - Pads must be securely distributed and protected at both sender and receiver ends.
  - The pad must be at least as long as the message to ensure security.

Running and Concealment Ciphers
- Running key cipher uses physical objects as keys (e.g., book pages, line, and column numbers).
- Concealment cipher or null cipher hides a message within a message using a pre-agreed method (e.g., every third word).

Steganography
- Method of hiding data within another medium, keeping the existence of the data secret.
- Can be used in various media types, including graphics, audio files, and documents.
- The Least Significant Bit (LSB) method modifies bits in a file without noticeable distortion or file size increase.

VERSAtile Reads

Main Components

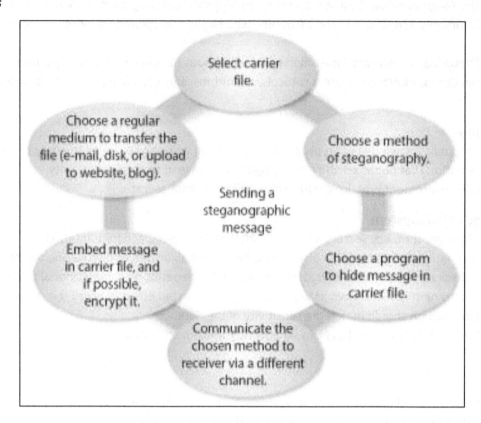

Types of Ciphers
- Symmetric encryption uses substitution and transposition ciphers.

Substitution Ciphers
- Replace bits, characters, or blocks with different ones as per a key (e.g., Caesar cipher).

Transposition Ciphers
- Scramble the order of characters or bits as determined by a key.

Symmetric Algorithms
- Utilize complex sequences of substitutions and transpositions.
- Algorithms define the processes, while keys dictate the specific order and methods used.
- **Algorithm and Key Relationship**
  - Algorithms consist of various "boxes" with mathematical formulas for encryption steps.
  - Keys add randomness by determining which boxes to use and their order.
- **Vulnerability to Frequency Analysis**
  - Simple substitution and transposition ciphers can be attacked through frequency analysis, identifying common patterns.
- **Key Derivation Functions (KDFs)**
  - Subkeys are created from a master key for individual use.
  - KDFs use hash, password, and/or salt values through several rounds of mathematical functions for security.

Methods of Encryption

- Encryption relies on complex algorithms and keys to convert plaintext into ciphertext.
- Two types of encryption: symmetric (secret keys) and asymmetric (public and private keys).

Symmetric vs. Asymmetric Algorithms

- Symmetric cryptography uses the same key for encryption and decryption.
- Asymmetric cryptography uses a pair of mathematically related keys for encryption and decryption.

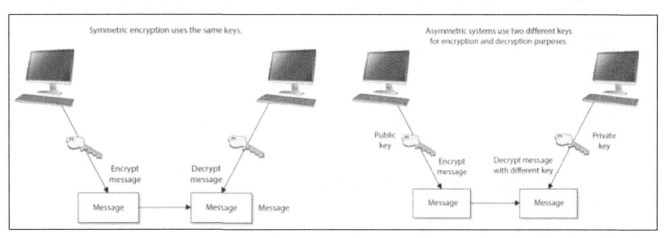

Symmetric Cryptography

- Users must keep the symmetric key a secret for security.
- Key management can be challenging with a large number of users due to the need for unique keys.
- Symmetric keys provide confidentiality but not authentication or non-repudiation.
- Complex to break with large key sizes.
- Example algorithms: DES, 3DES, Blowfish, IDEA, RC4, RC5, RC6, AES.

Block and Stream Ciphers

- Two main types of symmetric algorithms: block ciphers and stream ciphers.
- Block ciphers work on blocks of bits, while stream ciphers work on individual bits.

Block Ciphers

- Message divided into blocks, each encrypted with mathematical functions.
- Requires both confusion (complex substitution) and diffusion (scrambling of bits within blocks) for strength.
- **Strong block cipher:** change in one plaintext bit should affect about half of the ciphertext bits (avalanche effect).
- Utilizes S-boxes for substitution methods during encryption.
- The key dictates the randomness and complexity of encryption.

Stream Ciphers

- Treats data as a stream of bits, encrypting one bit at a time.
- Uses keystream generators to produce a random stream of bits XORed with plaintext.

- Less secure than block ciphers but more practical for real-time applications like VoIP.
- Requires a lot of randomness and unbiased keystream generation.
- A single computational error affects only the subsequent stream, unlike block ciphers, where it can make a block undecipherable.

Hybrid Encryption Methods
- Combines symmetric and asymmetric systems to leverage the strengths of both.

Characteristics of a Strong and Effective Stream Cipher
- Easy hardware implementation.
- Long periods without repeating patterns in keystream values.
- Keystream is not linearly related to the key.
- Statistically unbiased keystream (equal number of zeroes and ones).
- **Cryptographic Transformation Techniques**
  - Diffusion, confusion, avalanche, initialization vector(IVs) , and random number generation increase cryptographic strength.
  - Other techniques include compression, expansion, padding, and key mixing for enhanced security.
- **Asymmetric and Symmetric Algorithms Used Together**
  - Public key cryptography uses asymmetric algorithms for key distribution.
  - Symmetric algorithms are used for bulk data encryption.
  - Asymmetric algorithms encrypt the symmetric key for secure transmission.
  - Asymmetric encryption is slower due to complex math; hence, it's used on keys, not messages.

- **Digital Envelopes**
  - Combination of symmetric and asymmetric cryptography is also known as a digital envelope.
- **Session Keys**
  - Session keys are single-use symmetric keys for encrypting messages during a session.
  - A new session key is generated for each communication session to enhance security.

Types of Symmetric Systems
- DES, 3DES, AES, IDEA, Blowfish, and RC algorithms are symmetric encryption methods.
- Symmetric systems use the same key for both encryption and decryption.

Data Encryption Standard (DES)
- DES is a symmetric block encryption algorithm used historically for encryption.
- DES uses a 56-bit effective key length, which was eventually deemed insecure.
- DES has been replaced by the Advanced Encryption Standard (AES).

Triple-DES (3DES)
- 3DES enhances DES by encrypting data three times with different or the same keys.
- It is more secure but slower than DES due to more encryption rounds.

Advanced Encryption Standard (AES)
- AES, which uses the Rijndael algorithm, replaced DES.
- It supports key sizes of 128, 192, and 256 bits and has varying rounds based on key/block size.

International Data Encryption Algorithm (IDEA)
- IDEA operates on 64-bit blocks with a 128-bit key and is faster in software than DES.

Blowfish
- Blowfish encrypts 64-bit blocks with a variable key size up to 448 bits.
- It offers high performance due to its efficient algorithm design and simplicity, making it suitable for various encryption applications.
- It is unpatented and in the public domain.

RC 4
- RC4 is a common stream cipher with variable key size, used in Secure Sockets Layer (SSL) and initially in Wired Equivalent Privacy (WEP).

RC 5 & RC 6
- RC5 and RC6 are block ciphers with variable parameters for block size, key size, and rounds.

Cryptography Notation
- Shorthand notation (e.g., RC5-32/12/16) describes the configuration of the algorithm:
  - Word size in bits (w)
  - Number of rounds (r)
  - Key size in bytes (b)

Types of Asymmetric Systems
- Scalability issues arise with symmetric key cryptography due to the increased number of keys needed for more users.
- Secure key distribution requires a secure method to deliver the symmetric key to its destination.

Diffie-Hellman Algorithm:
- First asymmetric key agreement algorithm was developed by Whitfield Diffie and Martin Hellman.
- Allows two parties to generate a shared symmetric key by exchanging public keys.
- Vulnerable to man-in-the-middle attacks since it doesn't authenticate public keys before exchange.

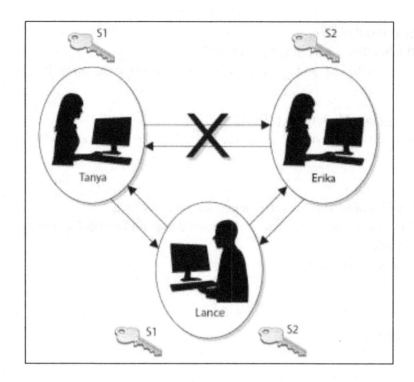

RSA
- Developed by Ron Rivest, Adi Shamir, and Leonard Adleman in 1978.
- Popular algorithm used for digital signatures, key exchange, and data encryption.
- Based on the difficulty of factoring large numbers into prime numbers.
- RSA keys are created from two large prime numbers.

El Gamal:
- Public key algorithm based on discrete logarithms in a finite field.
- Similar to Diffie-Hellman but slower in performance.

Elliptic Curve Cryptosystems (ECC):
- Utilizes smaller key sizes, which is advantageous for devices with limited resources.

Knapsack:
- Based on the knapsack problem, initially used for encryption.
- It was found to be insecure and is not currently in use.

Zero Knowledge Proofs
- Zero knowledge proof ensures that only the necessary information is revealed to verify a claim without divulging any additional details that could compromise security or privacy.
- This cryptographic technique allows individuals to prove possession of certain knowledge or credentials without exposing sensitive data, thus maintaining confidentiality and security.

Message Integrity
- Parity bits and CRC functions can detect only unintentional modifications in data transmission.

VERSAtile Reads

- One-way hash functions are required to detect both intentional and unintentional unauthorized data modifications.

The One-Way Hash
- A one-way hash produces a fixed-length hash value from a variable-length string.
- It ensures data integrity by allowing the receiver to compare a computed hash with the received hash.

Various Hashing Algorithms
- **Hash Algorithms**
  - Hash algorithms operate without keys and are publicly known.
  - They are one-way functions, meaning they are not meant to be reversed.
- **Hash-based Message Authentication Code (HMAC)**
  - An HMAC uses a symmetric key combined with the message.
  - It provides integrity and authentication, as only someone with the symmetric key can generate a valid MAC.
- **Cipher Block Chaining Message Authentication Code (CBC-MAC) and Message Authentication Code (MAC)**
  - Both use symmetric keys for authentication and integrity.
  - CBC-MAC uses a symmetric block cipher in CBC mode, while CMAC is a more secure variation.
  - They provide system authentication but not user authentication.

MD4 & MD5
- MD4 and MD5: No longer considered secure due to collision vulnerabilities.

SHA
- SHA stands for Secure Hash Algorithm. It is a cryptographic hash function used to generate a fixed-size hash value (often called a checksum) from input data of any size. SHA algorithms are commonly used in various security applications such as digital signatures, message authentication codes (MACs), and checksums to ensure data integrity and security.

- SHA-1: Found to be vulnerable to collisions.
- SHA-2 and SHA-3: Secure and recommended for use.

Attacks against One-Way Hash Functions
- Hash functions should be collision-free, meaning they shouldn't produce the same hash for different messages.
- Birthday attacks exploit statistical principles to find collisions.
- Key Points
  - Strong hash functions have a set of security characteristics, including resistance to birthday attacks.
  - Larger hash values are less vulnerable to brute-force attacks, which is why newer SHA versions have larger outputs.

Public Key Infrastructure (PKI)
- PKI is a framework enabling secure, trusted communication across various networks, including the internet.
- Uses public key cryptography and the X.509 standard for authentication.
- Provides authentication, confidentiality, nonrepudiation, and message integrity.

Difference between Public Key Cryptography and PKI:
- Public key cryptography refers to asymmetric algorithms.
- PKI includes many elements like users, certificates, keys, Certificate Authorities (CAs), and Registration Authorities (RAs), beyond just cryptographic methods.

Certificate Authorities (CAs):
- Issue digital certificates that contain an individual's public key and identity information.
- Bind an individual's identity to their public key and take on the liability for its authenticity.
- Allow secure communications between parties who trust the CA even if they haven't met before.
- Can be internal to an organization or external services like Entrust and VeriSign.
- Responsible for creating, maintaining, and revoking certificates.
- Use certificate revocation list (CRL) to revoke certificates, although Online Certificate Status Protocol (OCSP) is increasingly used for real-time validation.

Certificates
- Crucial for associating a public key with an entity.
- Created using the X.509 standard, which includes information like serial number, identity, and the CA's signature.

Registration Authorities (RAs)
- Handle certificate registration, confirm identities, and initiate the certification process with a CA.
- Act as a liaison between users and CAs but cannot issue certificates themselves.

PKI Steps
- Users request a certificate from an RA, which collects and verifies identification.
- The RA forwards the request to the CA after verification.
- The CA generates the certificate with the user's public key and sends it to the user.
- Users exchange certificates to obtain public keys for secure communication.
- **Entities and Functions in a PKI**
  - Includes CAs, RAs, certificate repositories, revocation systems, key backup and recovery, automatic key updates, key history management, timestamping, and client software.
- **Security Services Provided by PKI**
  - Ensures confidentiality, access control, integrity, authentication, and non-repudiation.
- **Key History**
  - A record of all old and current public keys used by individuals is essential.
  - Ensures that encrypted data can still be accessed even if it was encrypted with an old key.
- **Timestamping**
  - A reliable time source for secure timestamping is critical for true nonrepudiation.

Applying Cryptography
- Cryptography is vital for cyber security and has a limited shelf life; any cryptosystem can be broken with enough time and resources.

- The cryptographic life-cycle involves identifying cryptography needs, selecting algorithms, provisioning capabilities, managing keys, and updating systems as needed.
- Staying current with cryptologic research is crucial for early warnings about vulnerabilities in algorithms.

Services of Cryptosystems
- Cryptosystems provide confidentiality, integrity, authentication, authorization, and non-repudiation.
- Different sectors prioritize these services differently based on their needs, e.g., the military values confidentiality, while financial institutions value integrity.

Digital Signature
- A hashed message encrypted with the sender's private key ensures integrity, authentication, and non-repudiation.
- The recipient can verify the message by decrypting the digital signature with the sender's public key and comparing hash values.

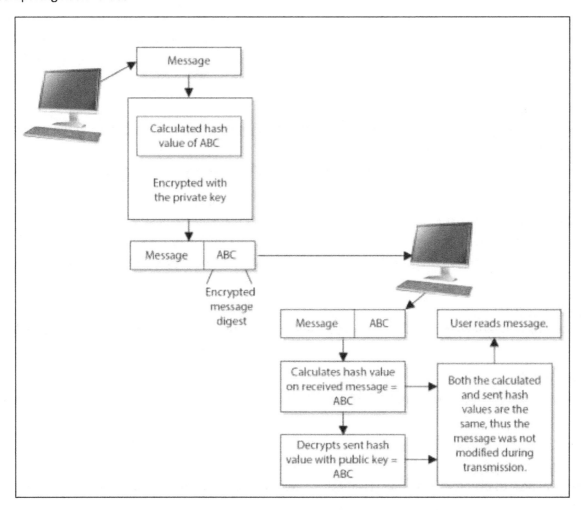

Digital Signature Standard (DSS)
- Established by NIST in 1991, DSS requires federal departments to use DSA, RSA, or ECDSA with SHA for digital signatures.

Key Management

- Key management involves securing keys during storage, transmission, generation, and destruction.
- Automated key distribution is preferred over manual processes for accuracy and security.
- Key management complexity and security are crucial; poor key management undermines even strong algorithms.
- **Key Management Principles**
  - Keys should be long enough, random, and have a suitable lifetime based on data sensitivity and usage frequency.
  - Key storage and transmission require secure methods.
  - Keys should be backed up and properly destroyed after use.

Trusted Platform Module (TPM)

- TPM is a hardware chip on motherboards providing secure storage and processing of keys, hashes, and certificates.
- It improves the Root of Trust and allows for secure system configurations (sealing and binding).
- **TPM Uses**
  - TPM binds a hard drive to a system, encrypting content and storing decryption keys within the chip.
  - TPM can seal a system to specific hardware and software configurations, ensuring system integrity.

Digital Rights Management (DRM)

- DRM controls access to copyrighted data using standard cryptographic technologies for authentication, authorization, and product key verification.
- DRM can be implemented without internet connectivity, and digital watermarks can help track unauthorized distribution.

Attacks on Cryptography

- Passive attacks: Eavesdropping or sniffing data without altering the encryption system; difficult to detect.
- Active attacks: Involves altering messages or system files; usually precedes passive attacks.

Ciphertext-Only Attacks

- Attacker has ciphertext and aims to discover the encryption key; which is common but challenging due to limited information.

Known-Plaintext Attacks

- Attacker has both plaintext and ciphertext; and uses known message parts to reverse-engineer the encryption key.

Chosen-Plaintext Attacks

- Attacker chooses plaintext and obtains ciphertext; gains deeper encryption process insight to determine the key.

Chosen-Ciphertext Attacks

- Attacker chooses ciphertext to decrypt and analyzes the plaintext; requires control over the decryption system.

Adaptive Attacks

- Derivative of the previously mentioned attacks; attacker refines subsequent attacks based on information from previous ones.

Differential Cryptanalysis

- Analyzes encryption of plaintext pairs with specific differences to uncover the encryption key; effective against some block algorithms.

Public vs. Secret Algorithms

- Public algorithms undergo peer review; private ones like those used by the NSA are not publicly scrutinized but are considered high quality.

Linear Cryptanalysis

- Known-plaintext attack variant; uses multiple messages to identify probable key through S-box input and output analysis.

Side-Channel Attacks

- The Attacker gathers external information (e.g., power consumption, radiation, timing) to infer the encryption key or sensitive data.

Replay Attacks

- Attacker resubmits captured data (e.g., authentication information) to trick systems; mitigated by sequence numbers and timestamps.

Algebraic Attacks

- Exploits mathematical vulnerabilities within the encryption algorithm's structure.

Analytic Attacks

- Targets structural weaknesses or flaws in the algorithm rather than using brute force.

Statistical Attacks

- Exploits statistical weaknesses in algorithm design, such as biases in a random number generator.

Social Engineering Attacks
- Tricks individuals into revealing cryptographic keys through persuasion, coercion, or bribery.

Meet-in-the-Middle Attacks
- Mathematical technique analyzing a problem from both ends by encrypting from one end and decrypting from the other.

Site and Facility Security
- Discussed computing architectures and system security evaluation.
- Emphasized the importance of cryptography for protecting information.
- Noted that system security is insufficient without physical security measures.
- **Importance of Physical Security:**
    - Physical access by attackers can lead to system compromise.
    - Physical security is often overlooked compared to technological security aspects.
    - Focuses on protecting against physical destruction, theft, environmental issues, and intrusion.
- **Categories of Threats:**
    - Natural environmental threats (e.g., floods, earthquakes, fires).
    - Supply system threats (e.g., power outages, communication disruptions).
    - Man-made threats (e.g., unauthorized access, vandalism, employee misconduct).
    - Politically motivated threats (e.g., terrorism, strikes).
- **Life Safety Goals:**
    - Human life is the highest priority in security planning.
    - Security measures must not hinder life safety, such as emergency exits.
- **Layered Defense Models:**
    - Implemented tiered physical controls from the perimeter to the assets.
    - Multiple layers provide backup if one fails (e.g., fences, walls, guards, IDS).
    - Inner layers protect the most sensitive assets.
- **Overall Security Objectives:**
    - Security protects all organizational assets and fosters a productive environment.
    - Aims to deter attackers by making the target less appealing.

The Site Planning Process
- A design team collaborates with management to create or improve a site and facility security program.
- Objectives are based on the organization's acceptable risk level, which is influenced by laws, regulations, and the organization's threat profile.
- Physical security combines people, processes, procedures, technology, and equipment to protect resources.
- The design process is methodical, considering objectives and resources.
- Organizations define vulnerabilities, threats, threat agents, and targets, distinguishing between internal and external threats.
- Performance metrics are essential for evaluating the effectiveness of physical security programs.
- **Similarities in Security Approaches**
    - Physical security program development follows similar steps to those for developing organizational security programs and business continuity plans.

- Each process requires a risk analysis to assess threats and risks, albeit with different focuses.
    - Steps include identifying a team, defining the scope, conducting a risk analysis, determining legal requirements, defining acceptable risk levels, establishing performance baselines, and implementing countermeasures.
- **Legal Requirements**
    - Compliance with regulatory and legal requirements is essential but often vague, necessitating expert consultation.
    - Case law also plays a role in determining physical security requirements.

Crime Prevention through Environmental Design (CPTED)
- A discipline focused on reducing crime by influencing human behavior through environmental design.
- Addresses landscaping, entrances, facility layouts, lighting, and traffic patterns.
- Strategies include natural access control, natural surveillance, and natural territorial reinforcement.

Designing a Physical Security Program
- The program is composed of various controls to meet policy and compliance requirements.
- Key considerations include construction materials, power distribution, communication pathways, external factors, and operational activities.
- The team must investigate and document current controls and identify weaknesses.
- Facilities should consider proximity to emergency services and environmental protection.
- Entry points like doors and windows require appropriate fortification based on threat assessments.
- Internal compartments, such as server rooms and data centers, should be centrally located and have strict access controls.
- Distribution facilities, storage facilities, and evidence storage must also be secure and meet specific requirements.

Internal Support Systems
- Physical security encompasses protecting assets and compartmentalizing areas and ensuring the functionality of essential support services like lights, air conditioning, and water supply within a facility.
- Notable incidents, such as the power outage affecting eight East Coast states and parts of Canada in August 2003, underscore the critical importance of addressing potential disruptions to power and other essential services.
- Security professionals must be prepared to mitigate both minor disruptions and major disasters to maintain organizational stability and security in the face of unforeseen events.

Electric Power
- Strategies for backup power to handle power failures due to various incidents.
- **Smart Grid**
    - Transition to smart grids with embedded computing for efficiency and reliability.
    - Smart grids are susceptible to cyberattacks due to increased technology integration.
- **Power Protection**
    - Use of Uninterruptible power supplies (UPSs) and power line conditioners to protect against power issues.

- Backup power systems and necessary for prolonged outages.
  - Regular testing of alternative power sources is essential.
- **Electric Power Issues**
  - Interference like EMI and RFI can disrupt power flow.
  - Power fluctuations can damage equipment and require voltage regulators for protection.
- **Preventive Measures and Good Practices**
  - Employ surge protectors and power line monitors.
  - Protect against magnetic induction and avoid daisy-chaining power strips by use shielded power cables and maintain a safe distance between electronic devices and magnetic sources to minimize the impact of magnetic induction and avoid daisy-chaining power strips to prevent overloading circuits and potential fire hazards, and instead use multiple outlets or surge protectors directly connected to a reliable power source.

Environmental Issues

- Importance of proper environmental controls to prevent hardware damage.
- Climate control in facilities, especially for computer systems, to prevent overheating.

Fire Prevention, Detection, and Suppression

- Adherence to fire safety standards and training.
- Use of early smoke or fire detection devices and proper suppression methods.
- **Types of Fire Detection**
  - Smoke and heat-activated detectors are crucial for early warning.
  - Proper placement of detectors is necessary above ceilings, below floors, and in ducts.
- **Fire Suppression**
  - Understanding of different fire types and appropriate suppression methods.
  - Different suppression agents are for different fire classes.
- **Water Sprinklers**
  - Water sprinklers are effective but can cause damage to electrical equipment.
  - Different types of sprinkler systems cater to varying requirements, with some designed to minimize water damage.

Mind Map

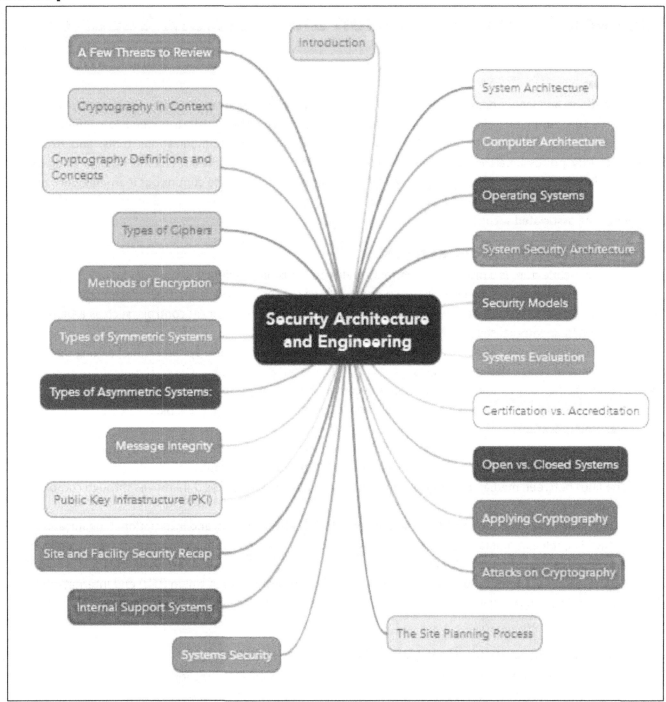

Chapter 05: Communication and Network Security

Introduction

Telecommunications and networking involve a complex interplay of mechanisms, devices, software, and protocols, compounded by the continuous emergence of new technologies. Network administrators need to configure software, protocols, and devices, address interoperability challenges, work with telecommunications tools, and troubleshoot effectively. Security professionals identify vulnerabilities in each component and understand how to mitigate them. Despite the challenges, possessing knowledge, practical skills, and a commitment to continuous learning opens numerous career opportunities in this ever-evolving field. This chapter provides an overview of networking and telecommunications basics, highlighting associated security issues.

Principles of Network Architectures

- Network architecture is a model that abstracts reality to focus on key details.
- It helps in making high-level decisions, such as identifying classes of servers and their placement.
- Different sets of servers (external, internal, developers) may require different controls, such as a Demilitarized zone (DMZ), an internal sharing cluster, and a development VLAN.
- Network architectures can serve as templates and best practices for future systems, emphasizing the importance of secure design principles.
- No one-size-fits-all solution; customization is necessary based on specific situations.
- CISSP professionals should be knowledgeable about various secure design principles.
- **Telecommunications**
  - Involves the electromagnetic transmission of data through various mediums, including copper wires, coaxial cables, airwaves, public switched telephone network (PSTN), and fiber cables.
  - The lines between media, technologies, protocols, and equipment blur as data moves through complex networks.
  - Typically include telephone systems and are regulated by governmental and international organizations.
  - In the U.S., telecommunications is regulated by the Federal Communications Commission (FCC), while in Canada, it's regulated by Industry Canada through System Integration & Test Terminal (SITT).
  - Global standards organizations like the International Telecommunication Union (ITU) and International Standards Organization (ISO), develop policies, recommend standards, and ensure technology compatibility.

Open Systems Interconnection (OSI) Reference Model

- Developed by ISO in the early 1980s for vendor-neutral network interconnection.
- The OSI model didn't become a protocol standard but is used as an abstract framework.
- Introduced after the basics of the internet and TCP/IP protocols were already in use.

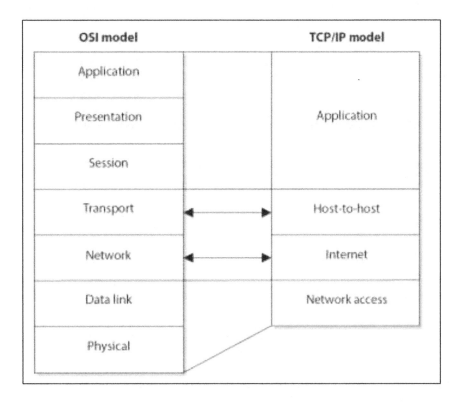

Protocol

- A set of rules for communication across networks, allowing different systems to understand each other.

Application Layer

- Protocols support applications; handles file transfers, message exchanges, etc.

Presentation Layer

- Data format translation, compression, and encryption; ensures interoperable data representation.

Session Layer

- Establishes, maintains, and ends connections between applications; session management.

Transport Layer

- Manages end-to-end data transport; reliable transmission, error detection, and flow control.

Network Layer

- Handles addressing and routing of packets; no guarantee of packet delivery.

Data Link Layer

- Frames data for transmission and translates data for LAN/WAN technologies.

VERSAtile Reads

Physical Layer
- Converts bits into voltage for transmission dealing with physical aspects of data transmission.

Multilayer Protocols
- Some protocols do not fit neatly into the OSI model, such as SCADA systems (DNP3) and vehicle systems (CAN bus).
- DNP3 lacks built-in security features; encryption and authentication were added later.
- CAN bus is vulnerable to attacks when vehicles are connected to external networks.

TCP/IP Model
- A suite of protocols for data transmission between devices, including TCP and UDP at the transport layer and IP for addressing and routing.
- IP is a connectionless protocol providing datagram routing services, like an addressed envelope in the postal system.

TCP
- Reliable, connection-oriented protocol ensuring packet delivery through handshaking, sequencing, flow control, and error correction.

UDP
- Best-effort, connectionless protocol without sequencing or flow control, suitable for applications where occasional data loss is acceptable.

Property	TCP	UDP
Reliability	Ensures that packets reach their destinations, returns ACKs when packets are received, and is a reliable protocol.	Does not return ACKs and does not guarantee that a packet will reach its destination. Is an unreliable protocol.
Connection	Connection-oriented. It performs handshaking and develops a virtual connection with the destination computer.	Connectionless. It does no handshaking and does not set up a virtual connection.
Packet sequencing	Uses sequence numbers within headers to make sure each packet within a transmission is received.	Does not use sequence numbers.
Congestion controls	The destination computer can tell the source if it is overwhelmed and thus slow the transmission rate.	The destination computer does not communicate back to the source computer about flow control.
Usage	Used when reliable delivery is required. Intended for relatively small amounts of data transmission.	Used when reliable delivery is not required and high volumes of data need to be transmitted, such as in streaming video and status broadcasts.
Speed and overhead	Uses a considerable amount of resources and is slower than UDP.	Uses fewer resources and is faster than TCP.

Port Types

- Well-known ports (0 to 1023) are standardized (e.g., port 25 for SMTP).
- Registered ports (1024 to 49151) can be registered with ICANN.
- Dynamic ports (49152 to 65535) are available for applications on an as-needed basis.
- **TCP Handshake**: Involves SYN, SYN/ACK, and ACK packets to establish a full-duplex virtual connection.
- **Data Structures**: Data encapsulation through the protocol stack with specific terminology (segment for TCP, datagram for UDP, packet for network layer, frame for data link layer).

IP Addressing

- IPv4 uses 32-bit addresses, with a host and a network portion.
- Addresses are grouped into classes and subnets with subnet masks to differentiate.
- Subnetting allows logical partitioning of networks for management, security, and traffic performance.
- Classful vs. classless addressing: Classless Inter-Domain Routing (CIDR) allows flexible IP address classes.
- Hostnames map to IP addresses for easier human recall, requiring a translation service (DNS).

IPv6

- Newer protocol with 128-bit addresses, built-in security features, scoped addresses, autoconfiguration, and does not require NAT.

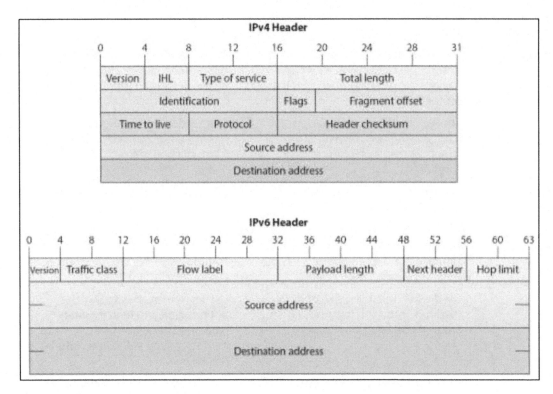

- Includes IEEE 802.1AE (MACsec) for data confidentiality and integrity, 802.1AR for unique device identifiers, and 802.1AF for key agreement.

Converged Protocols
- Protocols that have merged or can be encapsulated within another, such as Fibre Channel over Ethernet (FCoE), Multiprotocol label switching (MPLS), and, Internet Small Computer System Interface (ISCSI)

- IP convergence is the shift of various services onto IP-based transport.

Transmission Media
- Data is carried through electrical wires, optical fibers, or free space.
- Electrical wires use voltage changes, optical fibers use light properties, and free space typically uses radio signals.

Types of Transmission
- Analog: Data encoded onto carrier waves with varying amplitude and frequency.
- Digital: Data represented by discrete voltage values (1s and 0s), is more reliable and efficient than analog.
- Asynchronous: Data framed with start and stop bits, suitable for unpredictable data transmission.
- Synchronous: Data sent in a continuous stream with a common timing signal for synchronization, used for predictable, high-volume data transfers.
- **Bandwidth and Data Throughput:**
  - Bandwidth: The connection capacity, measured in bits per second, indicates the number of electrical pulses

that can be transmitted.

  - Data throughput: Actual amount of data carried over the connection, which can vary due to compression, congestion, or interference.

- **Broadband and Baseband**:
  - Baseband: Uses entire communication channel for a single transmission.
  - Broadband: Divides channel into subchannels for simultaneous, multiple data types transmissions.

Cabling

- **Coaxial Cable**: Copper core with shielding, better Equated Monthly Instalment (EMI) resistance, higher bandwidth, longer lengths than twisted-pair.
- **Twisted-Pair Cable**: Copper wires, can be shielded (STP) or unshielded (UTP), susceptible to interference and signal degradation over distance.
- **Fiber-Optic Cable**: Uses light waves, higher transmission speeds, lower attenuation, and is more secure than copper cables.
- **Cabling Problems**:
  - **Noise**: Interference from environmental factors that can distort signals.
  - **Attenuation**: Signal loss over distance due to resistance in the wire.
  - **Crosstalk**: Signals from one wire interfering with another due to magnetic fields.
- **Fire Rating of Cables**:
  - Cables must meet fire codes, especially in plenum spaces, to avoid toxic chemical production in case of fire.
  - Plenum-rated cables have special jacket materials for safety.
- **Security and Installation**:
  - Cables should be installed securely to avoid damage, tripping hazards, and eavesdropping.
  - In high-security settings, fiber-optic cables or pressurized conduits may be used.

Wireless Networks

- Broadband wireless signals occupy frequency bands shared with other technologies.
- Wireless communication involves transmitting information via radio waves.
- Higher frequency signals can carry more data but are more susceptible to interference.
- Wireless devices share the finite radio frequency spectrum, leading to potential collisions.
- Wireless networks use Carrier-sense multiple access with collision avoidance (CSMA/CA) for collision avoidance.
- Spread spectrum techniques distribute signals to use bandwidth efficiently.

VERSAtile Reads

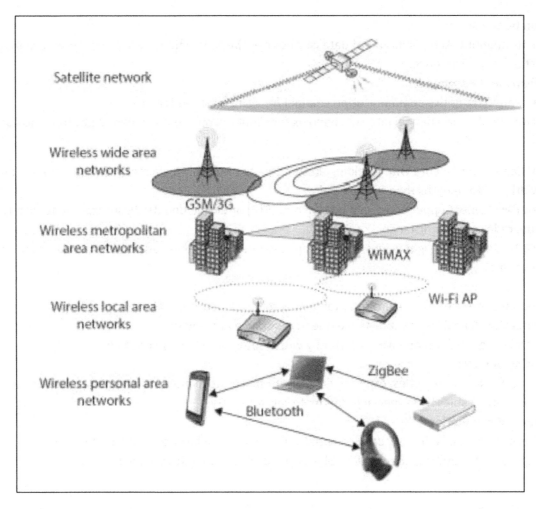

WLAN Components
- WLANs use Access Points (APs) to connect wireless devices to wired network resources.
- Infrastructure WLANs extend existing wired networks, while ad hoc WLANs have no APs, with devices connecting peer-to-peer.

Evolution of WLAN Security
- Original 802.11 standard's security flaws included poor authentication and static Wired Equivalent Privacy (WEP) keys.
- IEEE 802.11i or Wi-Fi Protected Access 2 (WPA2) improved security by using Advanced Encryption Standard (AES) and protocols like Temporal Key Integrity Protocol (TKIP).
- WPA2 provides encryption protection and is backward compatible with WPA devices.

Wireless Standards
- IEEE develops standards for interoperability; 802.11 was the first WLAN standard.
- Subsequent standards (e.g., 802.11a, 802.11b, 802.11g, 802.11n) provide different speeds and operate in different frequency bands.
- 802.16 (WiMAX) is a standard for broadband wireless Metropolitan Area Network (MANs).

- **Optical Wireless**
  - Combines Radio Frequency (RF) wireless and optical fiber, using laser systems Facility Security Officer (FSO) for point-to-point connections.
- **Bluetooth Wireless**
  - Enables low-range connectivity between devices, susceptible to attacks like bluejacking and bluesnarfing.

Best Practices for Securing WLANs
- Change default SSID, implement WPA2 with 802.1X, use VLANs, deploy WIDS, physically centralize APs, use VPNs, and restrict MAC addresses.

Satellites
- Provide broadband transmission for various services, with signals transmitted to and from satellites via ground stations.

Mobile Wireless Communication
- Has evolved through generations (1G to 4G) with increasing data rates and capabilities.
- Technologies like Frequency Division Multiple Access (FDMA), Time Division Multiple Access (TDMA), Code Division Multiple Access (CDMA), and Orthogonal Frequency Division Multiple Access (OFDMA) have been foundational to the evolution of mobile communication standards.

Networking Foundations
- Started with isolated mainframes and "dumb" terminals.
- Evolved in the late 1960s and early 1970s with the connection of mainframes and Unix systems.
- Ethernet development allowed for true networking, sharing resources, and increased computing power.

Network Topology
- Physical and logical layouts of networks vary.
- Ring topology: Devices form a closed loop, creating dependence between nodes.
- Bus topology: Single cable with nodes connected, susceptible to a single point of failure.
- Star topology: Nodes connected to a central device, less cabling, and easier to manage potential cable issues.
- Mesh topology: Nodes interconnected, providing redundant paths, used in IoT and the internet.

Media Access Technologies
- Define how systems communicate over media; reside at the data link layer of the OSI model.
  - LAN technologies set rules for communication, error handling, and frame size (MTU).
  - Technologies include Ethernet, Token Ring, Fibre Distributed Data Interface (FDDI), and wireless networks.
- Media Sharing
  - Token Passing: Used by Token Ring and FDDI; allows only the device with the token to communicate.
  - CSMA/CD: Used by Ethernet; nodes listen for a free cable to transmit data, collisions managed by a back-off

algorithm.
 - CSMA/CA: Used in Wi-Fi; signals intent to transmit to avoid collisions.
 - Carrier-sensing is faster than token-passing but prone to collisions.
 - Polling: Primary stations control when secondary stations transmit.
- LANs and WANs
 - LAN: Local network with specific cabling, protocols, and access technologies.
 - WAN: Connects LANs over greater geographical distances with different technologies.
 - Distinctions matter in terms of addressing, domains, and communication methods.
- Ethernet
 - Dominant LAN technology, evolved from 10 Mbps to 10 Gbps.
 - Uses CSMA/CD, supports full-duplex, and accommodates various cabling types.
 - Versions: 10Base-T, 100Base-TX, 1000Base-T, and 10GBase-T.
- Token Ring
 - Developed by IBM, uses a star-configured physical topology and logical ring signal path.
 - Employs token-passing for communication and has mechanisms for error handling.
- Fibre Distributed Data Interface (FDDI)
 - High-speed, token-passing, fault-tolerant technology using fiber-optic cables.
 - Provides primary and secondary rings for redundancy.
 - Used for backbone networks and can span up to 100 kilometers.

Transmission Methods
- **Unicast**: One-to-one transmission.
- **Multicast**: One-to-many transmission, managed by Internet Group Management Protocol (IGMP), for efficient resource usage.
- **Broadcast**: One-to-all transmission, used for messages to all systems on a subnet.

Network Protocols and Services
- Networks consist of various protocols and services, such as UDP, TCP, IP, IGMP, DHCP, and DNS.
- Every computer and network device requires a unique IP address and MAC address for communication.

Address Resolution Protocol (ARP)
- The Address Resolution Protocol (ARP) helps map IP addresses to the corresponding MAC address for communication on TCP/IP networks.
- ARP can be exploited in an attack known as ARP table cache poisoning, where an attacker redirects traffic intended for one computer to another.

Dynamic Host Configuration Protocol (DHCP)
- Assigns IP addresses to network clients in real time, preventing IP address conflicts.
- Attackers can masquerade as DHCP servers to compromise network configurations.
- DHCP snooping on network switches can prevent unauthorized DHCP clients and servers.
- Diskless workstations use Reverse Address Resolution Protocol (RARP) and Bootstrap Protocol (BOOTP) for network booting and obtaining IP addresses.

Internet Control Message Protocol (ICMP)
- Delivers status messages and reports errors.

- It's used in tools like ping and Traceroute but can also be exploited for attacks.

Simple Network Management Protocol (SNMP)
- Simple Network Management Protocol (SNMP) is used for network management but can expose networks to attacks if not secured properly.

Domain Name Service (DNS)
- Domain Name Service (DNS) translates human-friendly hostnames to IP addresses.
- DNS security measures like DNSSEC improve the authentication of DNS messages to prevent spoofing.
- Split DNS setups can enhance security by separating internal and external DNS queries.

E-mail Services
- E-mail services rely on SMTP for sending messages, with POP and IMAP protocols for mail retrieval.
- SMTP servers can be misused for spamming if relaying is not properly configured.

Network Address Translation (NAT)
- Network Address Translation (NAT) allows private IP addresses to communicate over the internet

- Can offer security by masking internal IP structures.

Routing Protocols
- Routing protocols manage the path of data across networks, with interior protocols like RIP, OSPF, IGRP, and EIGRP for routing within autonomous systems.
- Border Gateway Protocol (BGP) is an exterior routing protocol used between different autonomous systems on the internet.
- Routing protocols are subject to various attacks, such as spoofed ICMP messages and misdirecting traffic, which can be mitigated with authentication and encryption.

Network Components
- Devices used in LAN, MAN, and WAN for intercommunication among computers and networks.
- Types of devices include repeater, bridge, router, switch, gateway, firewall, proxy server and content distribution network.

Repeaters
- Simple connectivity devices that extend the network by repeating signals between cable segments.
- Work at the physical layer, amplifying signals and possibly cleaning them.
- Hubs are multiport repeaters that broadcast signals to all connected systems.

Bridges
- Connect LAN segments, working at the data link layer using MAC addresses.
- Filter frames, divide overburdened networks, and control traffic.
- Types include local, remote, and translation bridges.
- Use forwarding tables and Spanning Tree Algorithm for efficient frame forwarding.

Routers
- Operate at the network layer, connecting networks and routing packets based on IP addresses.
- Perform advanced functions like calculating shortest paths and fragmentation of datagrams.
- Use routing protocols like RIP, BGP, and OSPF.

Switches
- Combine repeater and bridge functionalities.
- Provide dedicated bandwidth and reduce traffic through direct device communication.
- Range from basic layer 2 to advanced multilayered switches with routing and traffic management capabilities.

Gateways
- Act as translators between different network environments or protocols.
- Examples include mail gateways and voice and media gateways.

Firewalls
- Restrict network access, acting as choke points.
- Types include packet filtering, stateful, proxy, dynamic packet filtering, kernel proxy, and unified threat management appliances.
- Architectures include dual-homed, screened host, and screened subnet.

Proxy Servers
- Act as intermediaries between clients and servers, controlling and filtering access.
- Types include forwarding, open, anonymous open, and reverse proxies.

Unified Threat Management (UTM)
- All-in-one appliances providing a range of security functionalities like firewalls, antimalware, IDS/IPS, and more.

Content Distribution Networks (CDN)
- Distribute content across multiple servers to optimize for users based on geographical location.
- Protect against DDoS attacks by distributing traffic.

Software Defined Networking (SDN)

- Centralizes network control and abstracts control and forwarding planes for dynamic and efficient traffic routing.

Endpoints

- Include devices like desktops, laptops, servers, smartphones, tablets, POS systems, IoT, and ICS devices.
- Require network access control to verify device configurations and compliance.

Honeypot

- A decoy system is set up to attract attackers, allowing administrators to study attack methods.

Virtualized Networks

- Networks that exist within virtual environments allow VMs to communicate over virtual switches and ports.
- Security relies on hypervisor integrity, patching, third-party add-ons, and competent administration.

Intranets and Extranets

- Companies use intranets for centralized business information and operational tools.
- Intranets are private networks that use web servers, client machines, and TCP/IP.
- Web-based clients on intranets restrict access to the system's resources and provide a standard GUI.
- Intranets utilize HTML/XML, accessed via HTTP, and are not platform-dependent.
- Extranets extend intranets to allow business-to-business sharing and collaboration.
- Extranets can pose security risks if not properly managed with firewalls and VPNs.
- **Value-Added Networks (VAN)**
  - EDI is used for internal and inter-company communication, often between retailers and suppliers.
  - VANs are EDI infrastructures managed by service bureaus for streamlined processing.
  - Retailers like Wal-Mart use VANs to automate inventory requests to suppliers.
  - EDI is transitioning from proprietary to standardized communication for better interoperability.
  - XML, SOAP, and web services are newer technologies used in supply chain infrastructures.

Metropolitan Area Networks (MAN)

- Connects Local Area Networks (LANs) and Wide Area Networks (WANs), the internet, and other networks.
- Often composed of Synchronous Optical Networks (SONETs), FDDI rings, or Metro Ethernet.
- **SONET**
  - Standard for telecommunications over fiber-optic cables.
  - Deployed by carriers and telephone companies primarily in North America.
  - Allows for intercommunication between different networks following SONET standards.

Metro Ethernet

- Ethernet can extend beyond LAN to cover metropolitan areas.
- Can be used as pure ethernet or integrated with technologies like Multiprotocol label switching (MPLS).
- Pure ethernet is cheaper but less reliable and scalable compared to MPLS-based Ethernet.

Wide Area Networks (WAN)
- WAN technologies span larger distances.
- WAN connects networks over long distances through routers and service provider infrastructure.

Telecommunications Evolution
- Began with copper-based analog systems and manual switching, progressing to electronic switching.
- Multiplexing allows multiple calls on one wire, with the illusion of a dedicated line.
- Digital phone systems with T1 and T3 trunks to increased call capacity and speed.
- Fiber-optics and SONET (Synchronous Optical Networking) further expanded call capacity.
- Asynchronous Transfer Mode (ATM) encapsulates data in fixed cells for delivery over SONET.

Dedicated Links
- **T-Carriers and E-Carriers**
  - T-carriers are dedicated lines like T1 and T3 for voice and data transmission.
  - T1 lines can carry 24 conversations, while T3 lines can carry up to 28 T1 lines.
  - E-carriers serve a similar function in Europe, with E1 and E3 lines as common standards.

- **Optical Carrier (OC)**
  - High-speed fiber-optic connections with OC levels (e.g., OC-1, OC-3, OC-12) indicating speed.
  - Used by companies and service providers for large bandwidth needs.

- **Multiplexing Types**
  - Statistical Time-Division Multiplexing (STDM): Transmits data simultaneously from multiple devices.
  - Frequency-Division Multiplexing (FDM): Uses frequency bands for multiple data transfer channels.
  - Wave-Division Multiplexing (WDM): Multiplexes optical signals on a single fiber.

WAN Technologies
- Channel Service Unit/Data Service Unit (CSU/DSU) required for LAN-to-WAN connections using T1/T3 lines.
- Switching can be circuit (dedicated path) or packet (dynamic paths) based.
- **Frame Relay**
  - A packet-switching WAN technology that allows shared use of carrier networks.
  - Virtual circuits (permanent or switched) provide paths for data frames.
  - Less costly than dedicated lines and allows for flexible bandwidth usage.
- **X.25**
  - An older WAN protocol with packet-switching used for connecting devices to networks.
  - Provides any-to-any connections with variable charges based on bandwidth usage.
- **Automated Teller Machine (ATM)**
  - High-speed cell-switching technology used for various network connections.
  - Data segmented into fixed-size cells for efficient and fast transmission.
  - Supports virtual circuits and Quality of Service (QoS) with guaranteed bandwidth.

- **Quality of Service (QoS)**
  - Provides priority levels for different classes of messages.
  - Ensures specific throughput and performance for time-sensitive applications.
  - Different levels include best-effort, differentiated, and guaranteed service.
- **Synchronous Data Link Control (SDLC) and High-Level Data Link Control (HDLC)**
  - SDLC is used in mainframe environments for communication with IBM hosts.
  - HDLC is an extension used for device-to-device communications in WANs.
- **Point-to-Point Protocol (PPP)**
  - Data link protocol for point-to-point connections.
  - Supports encapsulation of multiprotocol packets and provides authentication methods.
- **High-Speed Serial Interface (HSSI)**
  - Interface for connecting devices to high-speed communication services.
  - Supports speeds up to 52 Mbps and works at the physical layer.

Communications Channels

- Data is treated equally, but for voice, video, or interactive communications, packet jitter is problematic.
- Packet jitter is the variation in delay times between consecutive packets.

Multiservice Access Technologies

- Combine data, voice, and video over one transmission line for better performance and cost efficiency.
- **Public-Switched Telephone Network (PSTN)**
  - Circuit-switched network using Signaling System 7 (SS7) for call setup and teardown.
  - PSTN is being replaced by packet-oriented networks supporting voice, data, and video.
- **Voice over IP (VoIP)**
  - Uses Session Initiation Protocol (SIP) over TCP or UDP for call setup similar to SS7.
  - VoIP offers high-quality compression, uses IP addresses for numbers, and allows for intelligent end devices.
  - Latency delays and jitter are possible, but protocols aim to smooth out issues.
  - An isochronous network is needed for time-sensitive applications, ensuring continuous bandwidth.
- **Four Main Components of VoIP**
  1. IP telephony device (smartphone with necessary software).
  2. Call-processing manager.
  3. Voicemail system.
  4. Voice gateway for packet routing and access to legacy systems.
- **VoIP vs. IP Telephony**
  - VoIP refers to services like caller ID and QoS, while IP telephony encompasses all real-time apps over IP, including VoIP.

- **Call-processing manager vs Voicemail system.**

  - A call-processing manager oversees the routing and handling of incoming and outgoing calls within a telecommunications network, managing call flows and ensuring efficient call handling. In contrast, a voicemail system stores and manages recorded messages for users who are unavailable to answer incoming calls, providing a means for callers to leave messages that can be retrieved later by the intended recipient.

VERSAtile Reads

H.323 Gateways
- Part of Telecommunication Standardization Sector (ITU-T) recommendations for multimedia communications.
- Connects VoIP networks to PSTN and translates protocols.

Digging Deeper into SIP
- The signaling protocol used for initiating communication sessions in VoIP.
- Consists of User Agent Client (UAC) and User Agent Server (UAS).
- Relies on a three-way handshake process for session initiation.
- Includes proxy, registrar, and redirect servers for routing and maintaining user locations.
- **Skype**
  - Uses a peer-to-peer model rather than centralized servers for user directory maintenance.
- **Streaming Protocols**
  - Real-time Transport Protocol (RTP) is used for delivering audio and video over IP, usually run over UDP.
  - Real-Time Transport Control Protocol (RTCP) works with RTP for QoS feedback.

IP Telephony Issues
- VoIP faces similar security challenges as TCP/IP networks, such as unauthorized access and exploitation.
- Toll fraud and impersonation are significant threats.
- VoIP devices are vulnerable to DoS attacks and eavesdropping.
- **VoIP Security Measures**
  - Update patches, authenticate devices, and use firewalls, VPNs, and IDS/IPS.
  - Encrypt SIP packets with TLS to secure client/server communications.
  - Employ real-time monitoring and close media sessions after completion.

Remote Access
- Enables remote/home users to connect to networks via the internet.
- Reduces costs by using the internet instead of dedicated lines.
- Extends the workplace to remote devices.

Dial-up Connections
- Utilize existing telephone lines for network access.
- Modems convert digital signals to analog for transmission.
- Vulnerable to war dialing and unauthorized access.

Integrated Services Digital Network (ISDN)
- Digital technology for data and voice transmission over phone lines.
- Consists of Basic Rate Interface (BRI), Primary Rate Interface (PRI), and Broadband ISDN (BISDN).
- Offers higher bit rates and replaces aging analog systems.

Digital Subscriber Line (DSL)
- Provides high-speed internet over phone lines.
- Faster than ISDN with speeds up to 52 Mbps.
- Has limitations based on distance from the service provider.

Cable Modems
- Use existing cable TV infrastructure for internet access.
- Provide high-speed connectivity with shared bandwidth.
- Security concerns due to shared medium often mitigated by encryption.

Virtual Private Networks (VPNs)
- Secure, private connections over public networks.
- Use tunneling and encryption to protect data.
- Include different protocols like PPTP, L2TP, IPSec, and TLS.
- **Point-To-Point Tunneling Protocol (PPTP):**
  - Extends PPP connections over IP networks.
  - Used in client/server model and has security issues.
- **L2TP (Layer 2 Tunneling Protocol):**
  - Combines features of PPTP and L2F.
  - Supports multiple network types, beyond IP.
  - Used with IPSec for enhanced security.
- **IPSec (Internet Protocol Security):**
  - Suite of protocols to secure IP traffic.
  - Provides authentication, encryption, and integrity.
  - Works at the network layer for LAN-to-LAN connections.
- **TLS (Transport Layer Security):**
  - Provides session layer security for web and email traffic.
  - Embedded in browsers, easy to deploy.
  - Limited to specific application layer traffic types.

Authentication Protocols
- **Password Authentication Protocol (PAP):** Sends credentials in cleartext, least secure.
- **Challenge Handshake Authentication Protocol (CHAP):** Uses challenge/response for security.
- **Extensible Authentication Protocol (EAP):** Framework supporting various authentication methods.

Network Encryption
- Essential for protecting data confidentiality and integrity in modern networks.
- Utilizes encryption to safeguard email and web traffic.

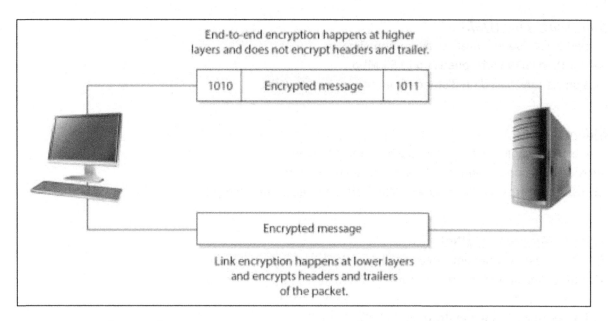

Link Encryption vs. End-to-End Encryption

- Link encryption encrypts all data along a communication path, including headers and routing information, but not data link control messaging.
- End-to-end encryption encrypts only the user data, leaving headers and routing information unencrypted.
- Link encryption provided by service providers, requires decryption at each hop.
- End-to-end encryption initiated by users stays encrypted from origin to destination.
- **Encryption at Different Layers:**
  - End-to-end encryption at the application layer.
  - TLS encryption at the session layer.
  - PPTP encryption at the data link layer.
  - Link encryption at data link and physical layers.
- **Advantages and Disadvantages:**
  - End-to-end encryption offers user flexibility and doesn't require decryption at each hop but leaves headers unprotected.
  - Link encryption secures all data, including headers, but makes key management complex and introduces more points of vulnerability.

E-mail Encryption Standards

- Standards ensure interoperability and have been heavily scrutinized.
- Companies need to decide on standards and technologies for encryption, taking into account cost-benefit analysis and resource availability.
- PGP and S/MIME are popular standards for e-mail encryption.
- **Multipurpose Internet Mail Extensions (MIME):**
  - Technical specification for transferring multimedia data and email binary attachments.
  - MIME specifies how files should be handled and transmitted.

- **Secure MIME (S/MIME):**
  - Standard for encrypting e-mails and attachments extends MIME.
  - Provides confidentiality, integrity, authentication, and non-repudiation.
- **Pretty Good Privacy (PGP):**
  - Freeware e-mail security program offering cryptographic protection.
  - Uses a web of trust instead of a hierarchical Certificate Authority (CA) model for key management.

Internet Security

- Protocols and software provide various services necessary for internet connectivity.
- Management determines allowed services, and administrators implement decisions through service control.
- **HTTP and HTTPS:**
  - HTTP is the protocol of the web, operating over TCP/IP.
  - HTTPS is HTTP running over SSL or TLS, adding encryption to web communications.
- **Secure Sockets Layer (SSL) and Transport Layer Security (TLS):**
  - SSL was developed by Netscape, now considered insecure and obsolete.
  - TLS is the standardized version of SSL, now the standard for secure transmissions.
- **Cookies:**
  - Text files maintained by browsers for various purposes, including advertising.
  - Can raise privacy concerns, though essential for some website functionalities.
- **Secure Shell (SSH):**
  - Provides terminal-like access and secure transmission for remote computers.
  - Uses a hand-shaking process and session key exchange for secure communications.

Network Attacks

- Networks are primary targets for cybercriminals, used for theft and espionage.
- Malformed packets were common early on; the "Ping of Death" is a notable example.
- Vigilant network monitoring and subscribing to threat feeds are key defenses against such attacks.
- **Flooding**
  - Overwhelming a target with packets, such as SYN flooding, which can incapacitate a server.
  - Modern defenses include rate-limiting features in routers and delayed binding techniques.

Denial-of-Service (DoS)

- Attacks disrupt service availability; keeping systems patched is crucial.
- **Distributed Denial of Service (DDoS)**
  - DDoS attacks use botnets to amplify attack volume.
  - Botnets can be rented, increasing the ease of launching massive DDoS attacks.
  - Content Distribution Networks (CDNs) and in-house traffic filtering are effective countermeasures.
- **Ransomware**
  - Ransomware encrypts user files, demanding payment for decryption.
  - Good network hygiene and awareness can reduce the risk of ransomware attacks.

Sniffing

- Network eavesdropping threatens data confidentiality.

- Sniffers require inside access to the network but can be detected if Network Interface Card (NIC) are in promiscuous mode.

DNS Hijacking

- Attackers redirect users to malicious DNS servers to conduct man-in-the-middle attacks or malware infections.
- Defenses include end-user computer hygiene, network intrusion detection systems, and secure DNS server configuration.

Drive-by Download

- Users can be infected by malware simply by visiting a compromised website.
- Keeping browser plug-ins patched and disabled by default can reduces the risk of drive-by downloads.

Mind Map

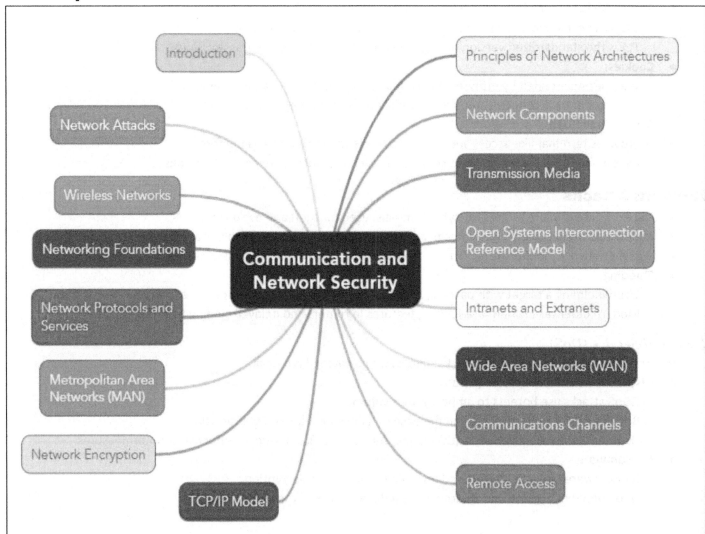

Chapter 06: Identity and Access Management

Introduction

The foundation of information security relies on controlling resource access to prevent unauthorized modification or disclosure. Access control measures can be technical, physical, or administrative and must be integrated into policy documentation, software, network design, and physical security. Access is a common target for exploitation as it serves as the gateway to critical assets. Implementing access controls in a layered defense-in-depth manner is crucial. This chapter explores access control concepts, delves into industry technologies enforcing these concepts, and examines common methods employed by malicious actors to attack these technologies.

Access Controls Overview

- Access controls are security measures that manage how users and systems interact with other systems and resources.
- They are used to prevent unauthorized access and are set after successful authentication.
- Subjects (active entities like users, programs, and processes) request access to objects (passive entities like computers, databases, and files).
- Access involves the transfer of information between a subject and an object.
- Access control mechanisms are vital as they are among the primary defenses against unauthorized system and network resource access.
- They verify user identities and grant permissions based on identities, clearances, or group memberships.
- Access controls help organizations control, restrict, monitor, and protect resource availability, integrity, and confidentiality.

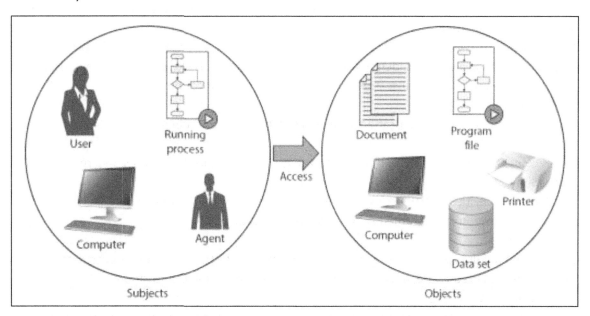

Security Principles

- Security management involves identifying threats to these principles and implementing countermeasures.

Availability
- Ensures timely access to information and resources for user productivity.
- Fault tolerance and recovery mechanisms are crucial for maintaining availability.
- Attributes of information like accuracy, relevance, and timeliness are important; privacy may be less so depending on context (e.g., stockbrokers).

Integrity
- Information must be protected from unauthorized alterations to ensure accuracy and completeness.
- Security mechanisms should alert users or administrators of any illegitimate modifications (e.g., altered banking transactions or sensitive emails).

Confidentiality
- Ensures information is not disclosed to unauthorized parties.
- Requires control mechanisms for access and dictates permissible actions with accessed data.
- Varies in sensitivity, necessitating different levels of protection (e.g., health records vs. daily specials in the cafeteria).
- Encryption, access controls, and monitoring are ways to maintain confidentiality.

Implementing Security Mechanisms
- Identifying the sensitivity and classification of data is the first step in protecting confidentiality.
- Security mechanisms must match the environment, data classification, and security goals.
- Proper evaluation prevents wasteful expenditure on inappropriate or unnecessary products.

Identification, Authentication, Authorization, and Accountability
- **Identification**:
  - Method by which a subject claims a specific identity such as username, account number, and email
  - Subjects provide identification information to access resources.
- **Authentication**:
  - Process of verifying a subject's identity, usually through credentials like passwords, keys, or biometric data.
  - Credentials are compared against stored information for authentication.
- **Authorization**:
  - After identification and authentication, a system determines if the subject has the necessary rights and privileges.
  - Access control mechanisms check if the subject may perform requested actions on a resource.
- **Accountability**:
  - Tracking user activities and enforcing actions taken within a system or domain.
  - Unique identification and recorded actions ensure accountability.
- **Race Condition**:
  - Occurs when multiple processes use a shared resource, leading to incorrect task execution order.
  - Can be exploited in software, allowing authorization steps before authentication.
- **Logical Access Controls**:
  - Technical tools that enforce identification, authentication, authorization, and accountability.
  - Embedded within various systems and applications, for instance, Single Sign-On (SSO): A logical access control mechanism that allows users to authenticate once and gain access to multiple systems or applications

without needing to re-enter credentials. SSO systems typically use authentication protocols like OAuth or SAML to verify user identity across different platforms.

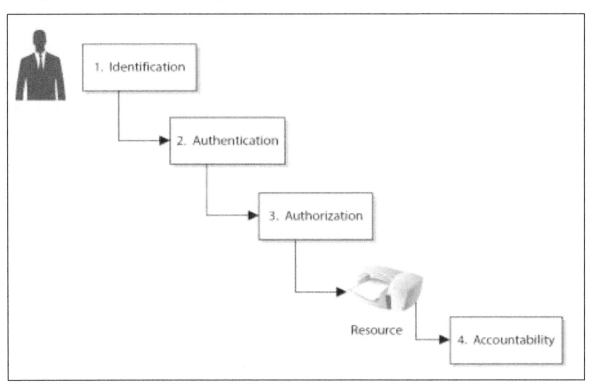

Identification and Authentication

- Strong authentication involves multiple factors
- **Identity Management (IdM)/Identity and Access Management (IAM):**
  - Encompasses automated user account management, access control, and auditing.
  - Centralizes and manages digital identities and their life cycles.
- **Directories:**

  Using directory services with permissions, access control lists (ACLs), and profiles
  - Contain network resources and user information.
  - Managed by directory services, following a hierarchical database format like X.500 with LDAP protocol.
- **Web Access Management (WAM):**
  - Software controlling user access to web-based enterprise assets.
  - Provides single sign-on capabilities and security for web services.

Authentication Methods

- **Credential Management Systems:**
  - Handle creation, modification, and deactivation of user accounts.
  - Include automated workflow for account approvals and provisioning.
- **Password Management:**
  - Includes password synchronization, self-service password reset, and assisted password reset mechanisms.
  - Reduces support calls and ensures secure password processes.

Authorization

- **Kerberos:** Uses tickets and symmetric key cryptography for authentication in client/server environments.
- **Security domains:** Group of resources under the same security policy. Authorization policies are often applied at the level of security domains to govern access to resources within a specific domain. Authorization decisions determine which users or groups are permitted to access resources within these domains based on defined security policies.
- **Directory services:** Authorization is managed and enforced through directory services, which centralize access control mechanisms. Directory services, such as Active Directory, LDAP, or AWS IAM, provide the infrastructure for defining and enforcing access rights, permissions, and roles across an organization's resources.
- **Thin clients:** Depend on central servers for processing and storage, providing a Single sign-on (SSO) solution. Authorization plays a crucial role in determining the level of access thin clients have to central servers for processing and storage. Authorization policies dictate which thin clients are allowed to access specific resources and perform certain actions within the centralized environment, ensuring security and compliance with organizational policies.

Accountability

- Auditing ensures accountability by tracking system, application, and user activities.
- Audit logs are used for security breach analysis, intrusion detection, and legal evidence.
- Protecting audit data involves strict access control and secure storage.

Session Management

- Establishes, controls, and terminates interactive communications between parties.
- Session can end due to timeout, inactivity, or anomaly detection.

Federation

- Federated identity allows authentication across business boundaries.
- Digital identity encompasses attributes, entitlements, and traits, forming a complex profile used for authentication and authorization processes.
- Identity management systems centralize identity information, including attributes like roles and clearances, entitlements, and traits, facilitating access control decisions.
- Federated identity management enables seamless sharing of user identity and authentication information across different organizations, enhancing user experience and security in online transactions and interactions.

Integrating Identity as a Service (IDaaS)

- IDaaS is a SaaS offering that provides Single Sign-On (SSO), federated Identity Management (IdM), and password management.
- It can be used for cloud-based and web-centric systems and legacy platforms in an enterprise network.
- **Architecting Identity Services:**
  - Two approaches: in-house (all systems/data within the enterprise) or outsourced (hosted by an external party).
  - Important to ensure compatibility and integration of all components.

On-premise

- Resources are controlled physically by the enterprise.
- Suitable for networks not directly connected to the internet, such as in critical infrastructure and military organizations.
- Requires expertise and time from the enterprise team for management.

Cloud

- Gartner predicts most new system purchases will use IDaaS by 2021.
- Regulated industries may face compliance issues with IDaaS.
- Security concerns arise when critical data moves outside of enterprise enclaves.
- Integration issues with legacy applications may need to be addressed.

Integration Issues

- Integration of technologies or products is complex and risky, requiring careful planning.
- Considerations include connectivity, trust, testing, and federation.
- **Establishing Connectivity:**
  - Secure communication between components is essential.
  - Different configurations are required for in-house vs. outsourced models, including firewall rules and network configurations.
- **Establishing Trust:**
  - Traffic must be encrypted, typically involving Public Key Infrastructure (PKI) and Certificate Authorities (CAs).
  - Trust issues may arise with internal CAs and outsourced services.
- **Incremental Testing:**
  - Important to test the integration incrementally to catch unforeseen issues.
  - Roll out to test accounts, then a single department, and finally the entire organization.
  - Use a testbed or sandbox environment for critical deployments.
- **Integrating Federated Systems:**
  - Assess connectivity with external organizations and ensure compatibility with the new IdM system.
  - Test and confirm that all external dependencies are accounted for and compatible.

Access Control Mechanisms

- Access control mechanisms dictate how subjects (e.g user) access objects (e.g files, systems).
- Utilize different models to enforce rules and objectives based on organization's needs.
- Five main types: discretionary (DAC), mandatory (MAC), role-based (RBAC), rule-based (RB-RBAC), and attribute-based (ABAC).

Discretionary Access Control (DAC)

- Resource owners define access based on their discretion.
- Implemented via Access Control Lists (ACLs).
- Common in operating systems like Windows, Linux, macOS, and Unix.
- Users can dynamically control access to their files.

- Vulnerable to malware as it operates under user's security context.

Mandatory Access Control (MAC)
- Does not allow users discretion over access.
- Used in highly secure environments like the military or government.
- Enforces strict structure with security labels indicating classification levels.
- Examples include SE Linux and Trusted Solaris.
- **Sensitivity Labels**
  - Required in MAC systems for every subject and object.
  - Contains classification and categories to enforce need-to-know rules.

Role-Based Access Control (RBAC)
- Centralized control based on user roles within an organization.
- Simplifies access control administration.
- Users are assigned roles which determine access rights.
- Can be combined with other access control models.

Rule-Based Access Control (RB-RBAC)
- Rule-based access control (RBAC) operates on specific rules dictating access permissions between subjects and objects, often expressed as "if X then Y" programming rules.
- RBAC, also known as RB-RBAC, complements traditional RBAC by providing finer-grained access control based on predefined rules that must be met before access is granted.
- Unlike identity-based access control models, rule-based access control applies universal rules affecting all users rather than individual identity-specific permissions, simplifying access management across the board.

Attribute-Based Access Control (ABAC)
- Attribute-based access control (ABAC) utilizes attributes from subjects, objects, actions, and contexts to define access permissions, providing granular control over access policies.
- Attributes such as clearance level, project affiliation, and time of day can be used to enforce specific access restrictions, allowing for highly customized and detailed access management.
- While ABAC offers extensive granularity in access control, the complexity of managing numerous interrelated policies can pose challenges, potentially leading to unforeseen interactions between policies.

Access Control Models
- DAC: Owners decide access, ACLs enforce decisions.
- MAC: OS enforces policy, and uses security labels.
- RBAC: Based on roles and positions.
- RB-RBAC: RBAC with additional rules.

Access Control Techniques and Technologies

- Types include menus and shells, database views, and physically constrained interfaces.
- Traditional authentication protocols include PAP, CHAP, and EAP.
- **Remote Authentication Dial-In User Service (RADIUS)**
  - A network protocol for client/server authentication, authorization, and auditing.
  - Used by ISPs and for corporate remote access, maintaining user profiles in a central database.
- **Terminal Access Controller Access Control System (TACACS)**
  - Evolved through three generations: TACACS, XTACACS, TACACS+.
  - TACACS+ offers more protection with dynamic passwords and encrypts all data between client and server.
  - Provides more granular control over user profiles and commands they can execute.
- **Diameter Protocol**
  - An advanced Authentication, Authorization, and Accounting (AAA) protocol that builds upon RADIUS to address its limitations.
  - Supports modern network demands such as wireless authentication and Mobile IP.
  - Provides a common framework for various services and better error detection and resilience.

Constrained User Interfaces

- Constrained user interfaces limit user access by restricting available functions or system resources.

Remote Access Control Technologies

- Remote access control technologies use Authentication, Authorization, and Accounting (AAA) protocols.

Access Control Matrix

- A table showing what actions subjects can take on objects.
- Implemented as table lookups by the operating system, indicating capabilities or ACLs.
- **Capability Table**
  - Details the access rights a subject has regarding specific objects.
- **Access Control Lists (ACLs)**
  - Lists indicating authorized users for a specific object and their level of access.
  - Mapped from the access control matrix to the object.

Content-Dependent Access Control

- Access is determined by the content within the object, such as database fields or email filters.

Context-Dependent Access Control

- Makes access decisions based on the collection of information.
- Examples include stateful firewalls and software that tracks a user's access sequence to prevent inference of sensitive information.

Managing the Identity and Access Provisioning Life-Cycle

- Involves creating user or system accounts as part of onboarding.
- Accounts should be periodically reviewed and deprovisioned as necessary.

Provisioning
- Requires an established process with HR, supervisor, and IT approvals.
- Answers the question of why an account is created, influencing future account activity.

  - The creation of an account serves as a foundational step, shaping the subsequent activities and interactions associated with that account.

  - It addresses the fundamental question of why the account exists, guiding decisions and actions taken within the account's scope.

  - Understanding the purpose behind account creation informs and influences future account usage patterns and behavior.

User Access Review
- Ideally integrated with HR procedures and triggered by specific administrative actions.
- Consider various conditions like extended leave, hospitalization, or investigations.

System Account Access Review
- System accounts require periodic reviews similar to user accounts but without HR involvement.
- Reviews prevent forgotten accounts from becoming security vulnerabilities.
- Software updates may render some system accounts obsolete, requiring deprovisioning.

Deprovisioning
- Accounts are eventually deprovisioned, typically as part of termination procedures.
- For system accounts, deprovisioning may occur due to system removal or configuration changes.
- It is important to document deprovisioning to stop tracking the account.
- Resource ownership should be transferred to avoid orphaned resources hindering business operations.

Controlling Physical and Logical Access
- Physical security includes guards, fences, secure server rooms, and access-restricted work areas.
- These controls handle logical system access, including operating systems, encryption, and network devices.

Access Control Layers
- Access control is categorized into administrative, technical, and physical controls.
- Controls function at different network layers and system levels, needing synergy for effective security.

Administrative Controls
- Senior management sets security goals and constructs the security policy foundation.
- Personnel controls govern employee interactions with security measures and address compliance.
- A supervisory structure ensures each employee has a superior responsible for their conduct.
- Security-awareness training educates employees on proper access and security protocols.

- Testing of security controls and procedures ensures alignment with security goals and policy.

Physical Controls

- Network segregation physically or logically separates network areas based on clearance or role.
- Perimeter security controls access to facilities through guards, badges, surveillance, and barriers.
- Computer controls include locks and device configurations to prevent unauthorized access or theft.
- Work area separation restricts access to sensitive locations within a facility.
- Cabling is shielded and routed to protect against interference and eavesdropping.
- Control zones divide facilities based on sensitivity, dictating different access control levels.

Technical Controls

- System access is managed through authentication methods such as passwords, biometrics, or smart cards.
- Network architecture logically segregates and protects different network segments.
- Network access is enforced by routers, switches, and firewalls, controlling segment-to-segment communication.
- Encryption and protocols secure data in transit and enforce communication pathways.
- Auditing tools monitor and record network and system activities for security analysis and improvements.

Access Control Practices

- Ensure no access for undefined or anonymous accounts.
- Limit and monitor privileged accounts.
- Suspend access after failed login attempts.
- Remove obsolete user accounts promptly.
- Suspend inactive accounts after 30-60 days.
- Implement strict access criteria and least privilege policies.
- Disable unnecessary system features, services, and ports.
- Change default passwords and enforce password policies.
- Monitor and restrict global access rules.
- Remove redundant access rules and accounts.
- Regularly audit system and user events.
- Protect audit logs to maintain integrity.

Unauthorized Disclosure of Information

- Information can be disclosed intentionally or unintentionally, often leading to unfavorable outcomes.
- Attacks like social engineering, malicious code, and electrical sniffing can cause unauthorized disclosure.
- Accidental disclosure can occur through object reuse without proper data clearing.
- **Object Reuse**
    - Formatting only removes file pointers, not the actual files.
    - Sensitive data classification and strict control over storage and access are crucial.
    - Before reuse, erase or degauss sensitive information on used media, or properly destroy it if purging is not feasible
- **Emanation Security**
    - Electronic devices emit signals that can potentially be intercepted.

- Intruders can use equipment to capture data from these emissions.
- Countermeasures include TEMPEST standards and equipment.
- **TEMPEST**
  - A Dial On Demand (DoD) study turned standard for countermeasures against spurious electrical signals.
  - Equipment is shielded, often with a Faraday cage, to suppress signal emanations.
  - Used primarily by military and other high-security organizations.
- **Alternatives to TEMPEST**
  - **White Noise**: Random electrical signals distributed over a full spectrum to mask real data.
  - **Control Zone**: Use of materials in walls to create a large Faraday cage containing signals within a secured perimeter.

Access Control Monitoring

- Tracks attempt to access company resources.
- Essential for internal network security.
- Goes beyond antivirus and firewall solutions.

Intrusion Detection Systems (IDS)

- Detect unauthorized use or attacks on computer systems and networks.
- Alert network managers of suspicious activities.
- Two types: network-based (NIDS) and host-based (HIDS).
- Components include sensors, analyzers, and administrator interfaces.
- Use pattern recognition, stateful matching, and anomaly detection.
- **Network-Based IDS (NIDS)**
  - Uses sensors in promiscuous mode to monitor all network traffic.
  - Cannot see inside a computer system.
- **Host-Based IDS (HIDS)**
  - Installed on individual workstations/servers.
  - Monitors internal computer activities.
  - Usually only on critical servers due to resource overhead.
- **Signature-Based Intrusion Detection**
  - Relies on known attack signatures for detection.
  - Must be regularly updated.
  - Ineffective against new, unknown attacks.
- **State-Based IDS**
  - Monitors state transitions in systems or applications.
  - Rules indicate which transitions should trigger alerts.
- **Statistical Anomaly–Based IDS**
  - Behavioral-based, learns "normal" activities to build a profile.
  - Alerts triggered by deviations from the established profile.
  - Can detect new "zero-day" attacks but is prone to false positives.
- **Protocol Anomaly–Based IDS**
  - Monitors for anomalies in protocol behavior.
  - Profiling combines official and real-world protocol usage.

- **Traffic Anomaly–Based IDS**
    - Detects unusual network traffic patterns.
    - Helps identify DoS attacks and new network services.
- **Rule-Based IDS**
    - Uses IF/THEN rules within expert systems.
    - Applies artificial intelligence characteristics.
    - Cannot detect new attacks without updated rules.
- **Application-Based IDS**
    - Monitors specific applications for malicious activities.
    - Limited to the application being monitored.
- **IDS Sensors**
    - Placed on network segments to monitor and report activities.
    - Critical to configure sensor placement effectively.

Intrusion Prevention Systems (IPS)

- Designed to prevent attacks, not just detect them.
- Can be host-based or network-based.
- **Honeypot**
    - A decoy system to attract attackers away from real systems.
    - Legal considerations should be taken into account.
- **Intrusion Responses**
    - IDSs can kill connections, block users, and send alerts.
- **Network Sniffers**
    - Programs/devices that examine traffic on a LAN.
    - Require promiscuous mode network adapters.
    - Used for both legitimate monitoring and malicious activities.

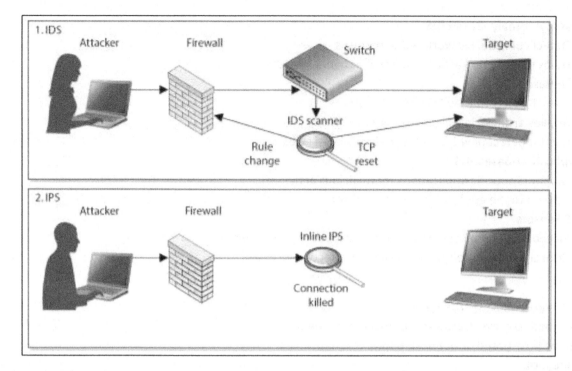

Threats to Access Control

- Insider threats often pose more risk than outsiders as they have legitimate access and intimate knowledge of the system.
- Specific attacks can be carried out by both insiders and outsiders.

Dictionary Attack

- Uses common words or character combinations to match hashed passwords.
- Countermeasures include using complex passwords, frequent rotation, and encryption.

Brute-Force Attacks

- Tries every possible combination of characters to uncover passwords.
- Often used with dictionary attacks for efficiency.
- Countermeasures involve lockout thresholds and monitoring for suspicious activity.

Spoofing at Log-on

- Fake login screens trick users into giving away credentials.
- Users may receive a fake error message and then the real OS prompt, leading them to believe they mistyped their information.

Phishing and Pharming

- Phishing lures individuals to reveal personal or financial information via deceptive emails or websites.
- Pharming redirects users to fraudulent websites by DNS poisoning.

- Countermeasures include skepticism towards unusual emails, manual URL entry, and TLS connections.
- **Spear-Phishing**:
  - A targeted attack using personal information to trick specific individuals.
  - More convincing due to personalized approach.
- **Countermeasures to Common Attacks**:
  - Use encryption and hashing for password storage and transmission.
  - Implement one-time passwords and Intrusion Detection System (IDS).
  - Educate users on how to recognize and react to phishing attacks.
  - Regularly update security practices to counter new attack strategies.

Mind Map

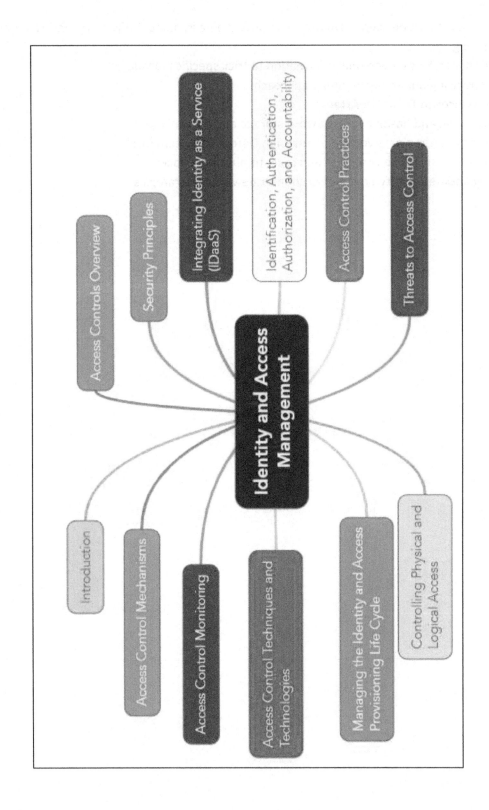

Chapter 07: Security Assessment and Testing

Introduction

Regularly assessing the effectiveness of security measures is crucial for maintaining a secure organization. Despite having skilled personnel, robust policies, and advanced technology, security can become compromised over time. This chapter highlights key elements of security assessments and testing. It emphasizes the importance of continuous evaluation to prevent security posture from becoming ineffective. The content covers assessment, testing, and audit strategies, considering the use of internal auditors versus external contractors. It also explores testing technical and administrative controls, primarily implemented through policies. The chapter concludes by discussing reporting findings and their role in executive decision-making within the organization.

Assessment, Test, and Audit Strategies

- Tests record and compare properties or behaviors against standards.
- Assessments are related series of tests to determine system security.
- Audits are systematic and check compliance with external standards.
- **Information System Security Audit Process**
  - Identify audit goals for focused effort.
  - Engage business unit leaders for relevant risk identification.
  - Scope the audit to cover specific systems, behaviors, and information.
  - Decide on an internal or external audit team based on expertise and requirements.
  - Plan the audit to meet goals efficiently.
  - Execute the audit, document deviations, and ensure repeatability.
  - Thoroughly document results for a detailed security posture snapshot.
  - Communicate results effectively to the right stakeholders.

Internal Audits

- Utilize familiar internal personnel for audits.
- Internal audits can quickly adapt to changing security needs.
- Potential downsides: limited exposure to varied security approaches and possible conflicts of interest.
- **Conducting Internal Audits**
  - Best practices include ensuring resource availability, preparing auditors, documenting everything, and creating readable reports.

External Audits

- External audits are contractually obligated and help ensure partners maintain security standards.
- In the wake of incidents like the Target breach, auditing partners' security practices is critical.
- **Conducting and Facilitating External Audits**
  - Understand contractual obligations.
  - Conduct in-and out-briefs to clarify audit scope and address issues.

- Accompany auditors to facilitate the process and prevent misunderstandings.

Third-Party Audits

- Often required for regulatory compliance.
- Advantages include varied experience and objective assessments.
- Disadvantages include high costs and the need for orientation and supervision.
- **Facilitating Third-Party Audits**
  - Know audit requirements and conduct pre-audits.
  - Schedule appropriately and organize resources.
  - Keep senior management informed of the audit process and potential issues.

Test Coverage

- Measure of how much of a system is tested, usually expressed as a percentage.
- Full coverage is often too costly, except for critical systems.
- Test coverage can be spread over time to achieve full annual coverage without overwhelming resources at once.

Auditing Technical Controls

- Technical controls are security measures implemented through IT assets.
- Auditing checks the control's effectiveness against identified risks.
- Understanding the context and intended purpose of controls is crucial.

Vulnerability Testing

- Involves both manual and automated processes to identify system vulnerabilities.
- Requires highly trusted staff with deep security knowledge.
- Management must provide a written agreement before testing
- Goals include evaluating security posture, identifying vulnerabilities, and testing system reactions to attacks.

Penetration Testing

- Simulates attacks to measure an organization's resistance and uncover weaknesses.
- Tests are extensive and may include web servers, DNS servers, routers, and more.
- Test types vary from black, white, to gray box testing, each with different levels of system knowledge.
- Penetration testing follows a five-step process: discovery, enumeration, vulnerability, mapping, exploitation, and reporting to management
- Different types of penetration tests are conducted based on the organization's security objectives.

Other Vulnerability Types

- Identify a range of vulnerabilities which can be used for foundation of penetration testing.
- The result is a report for management detailing vulnerabilities and remediation suggestions.

Postmortem

- A review of tests to determine remediation strategies and ensure mitigations are on track.

Log Reviews

- Examination of system logs to detect security events or verify controls.
- Requires event types to be carefully defined and timestamps to be synchronized using protocols like Network Time Protocol (NTP)
- Centralized logging is beneficial for analysis and archiving.
- Measures like remote logging, simplex communication, replication, write-once media, and cryptographic hash chaining can help prevent tampering.

Synthetic Transactions

- Scripted transactions to systematically test system behavior and performance.
- Can be used for testing new services and implementing security controls.
- **Real User Monitoring vs. Synthetic Transactions:**
  - RUM captures actual user interactions with systems passively.
  - Synthetic transactions are predictable and scripted, allowing for proactive monitoring.

Misuse Case Testing

- Use cases describe expected system behavior, while misuse cases describe potential threat actions.
- Useful for ensuring effective security controls are in place.

Code Reviews

- Software examination by a third party to ensure compliance with coding standards and security policies
- Includes looking for unnecessary functions, repeated code, and defensive programming techniques.

Code Testing

- Conducted before software moves to production to ensure security policy compliance.
- Part of the broader certification and accreditation process for software systems.

Interface Testing

- Evaluation of data exchange points between systems and/or users.
- Interface testing, a form of integration testing, evaluates how different system components interact.

Auditing Administrative Controls

- Administrative controls, implemented through policies or procedures, are vital and need to be audited by collecting security process data.
- Sophisticated threat actors often exploit administrative controls.

Account Management

- Attackers aim to gain normal privileged user status through compromised, created, or elevated privileged accounts.
- Strong authentication and vigilant account creation/modification are key defenses.
- **Adding Accounts**
  - New employees go through a process ensuring understanding of duties and responsibilities.
  - Must acknowledge understanding of policies such as the Acceptable Use Policy (AUP).
  - Cross-checking AUPs with user accounts verifies effective communication between HR and IT.
- **Modifying Accounts**
  - Changing user privileges should be a controlled process, documented with effective dates, reasons, and authorizations.
  - Privilege accumulation should be avoided; privileges must match roles.
- **Running as Root**
  - Using a restricted account for daily work and elevating privileges only when necessary is safer.
  - Different operating systems have various methods for privilege elevation.
- **Suspending Accounts**
  - Suspend unused accounts should be suspended to prevent unauthorized access.
  - Accounts should only be deleted in accordance with the data retention policy.

Backup Verification

- Backups must be tested to ensure data recovery is possible in case of disaster.
- Types of data like user files, databases, and mailbox data have unique backup considerations.
- Virtualization and snapshots are used for quick restoration and security.
- **Testing Data Backups**
  - Develop scenarios and a plan to test mission-critical data backups.
  - Automate testing to cover all systems with minimal business disruption.
  - Document results and address any issues found.

Disaster Recovery and Business Continuity

- Organizations need plans for business continuity and disaster recovery.
- Regular exercises are more productive than tests, revealing improvements and efficiencies.
- Testing drills prepare personnel and highlight plan deficiencies.
- **Testing and Revising the Business Continuity Plan (BCP)**
  - The BCP should incorporate a Disaster Recovery Planning (DRP) and be tested regularly.
  - A variety of drills can be conducted, ranging from checklist tests to full-interruption tests.
- **Emergency Response**
  - Proper training and drills are crucial for effective emergency response.
  - Protecting life is the primary concern before attempting to save material objects.
- **Maintaining the Plan**
  - BCPs can quickly become outdated; regular maintenance is crucial.
  - Integrating BCP into change management processes ensures it remains current.

Security Training and Security Awareness Training
- Both types of training are crucial, with security training focused on specific skills and awareness training on exposure to security issues.
- **Social Engineering**
  - manipulates individuals to breach security protocols.
  - Phishing, pretexting, and other forms are common and must be countered by awareness programs.
- **Online Safety**
  - Safe online behavior, especially on social media, is key to organizational security.
  - Awareness programs should educate users on the risks of unsafe online activities.
- **Data Protection**
  - Awareness programs should stress the importance of data protection.
  - Sensitive data should always be encrypted and securely destroyed when no longer needed.
- **Culture**
  - A security-aware culture is one where users feel safe to report incidents and seek guidance.

Key Performance and Risk Indicators
- KPIs and KRIs are used to measure the effectiveness of Information Security Management System (ISMS) and assess potential risks, respectively.
- They are essential for continuous improvement and informed decision-making regarding security management.

Reporting
- Considered critical but often disliked by security professionals.
- Distinguishes true security professionals, who can communicate technical details to both technical and non-technical audiences.
- Technical reports written for non-technical decision-makers must be technically sound and presented in business language.

Analyzing Results
- A three-step process:
  - First, gather and organize data to establish facts.
  - Second, assess the business impact of the facts.
  - Third, provide actionable recommendations considering the broader organizational needs.

Writing Technical Reports
- Should tell a compelling story beyond automated scanning tool outputs.
- Must be truthful and based on empirical facts.
- Key elements:
  - Executive Summary
  - Background
  - Methodology
  - Findings
  - Recommendations
  - Appendices.

- Raw data and analysis must justify recommendations.

Executive Summaries
- Translate technical findings and recommendations for senior leadership.
- Highlight risk exposure and potential savings for the company.
- Quantify risk in monetary terms using cost, income, and market approaches.
- Consider the life-cycle costs of controls versus mitigated risks, factoring in the effectiveness of controls.
- **Considerations for Senior Leaders**
  - Senior leaders are interested in effectiveness, cost savings, and total costs.
  - Technical details are more relevant to the ISMS team but indirectly important to business leaders.
  - Effective communication in reports is crucial for securing executive support and resources.

Management Review and Approval
- Involves senior leaders in assessing whether management systems, like the ISMS, meet their goals.
- They follow the Plan-Do-Check-Act loop from quality standards such as ISO 9000.
- Strategic decisions are made during these reviews rather than delving into technical details.

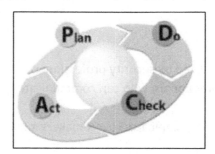

Before the Management Review
- Reviews should be periodic, with frequency depending on system and organization maturity.
- The timing should allow for the implementation and assessment of previous review decisions.
- Regularity ensures a proactive approach to decision-making.

Reviewing Inputs
- Inputs include audit results, summaries in business language, and the status of previous action items.
- Customer feedback, from direct sources or social media, informs the review.
- Recommendations for improvement are based on these inputs, focusing on high-level changes.

Management Approval
- Senior leaders consider inputs, debate, and decide whether to approve, amend, reject, or defer recommendations.
- The effectiveness of the ISMS team is judged by the leadership's response to their proposals.
- Outcomes of the review include a list of deliverables for the next session, continuing the improvement cycle.

Mind Map

Chapter 08: Security Operations

Introduction

Security operations involve the ongoing efforts to maintain secure and protected networks, computer systems, applications, and environments. This includes managing access privileges, monitoring, auditing, and reporting controls. Operations occur post-network development, focusing on routine activities to ensure continuous secure functioning.

Networks and computing environments evolve, requiring regular updates and monitoring. Companies often seek security consultants for infrastructure improvement, spending significant sums on suggested measures like firewalls and antivirus systems. However, the effectiveness of these measures relies on continuous updates, patching, monitoring, and vulnerability testing. Neglecting operational security tasks can lead to lapses in security. Despite thorough perimeter monitoring, threats may compromise information systems. Security operations also encompass detection, containment, eradication, and recovery to ensure business continuity and address liability and compliance issues. In the introduction section for other chapters, more information was mentioned regarding the content of the chapter

Role of the Operations Department in Security

- **Due Care and Due Diligence**: Emphasizes the need for companies to behave as a prudent person would by being responsible and cautious to maintain the right level of security.
- **Balance of Security Measures**: Companies must balance between security, usability, compliance, and cost.
- **Continual Security Maintenance**: Security operations focus on continuous efforts to keep the security of people, applications, equipment, and environments at the required levels.
- **Legal and Liability Concerns**: Organizations and their executives have legal obligations to ensure the protection of resources and the effectiveness of safety measures.
- **Threat Identification**: Companies must identify sensitive systems requiring protection from disclosure and critical systems requiring constant availability.
- **Context of Security Responsibilities**: These include adhering to legal, regulatory, and ethical standards
- **Physical and Environmental Security**: Controlling physical aspects such as temperature humidity, and securely disposing of media containing sensitive information is crucial for operational security.
- **Operational Security Components**: Includes configuration, performance, fault tolerance, security, and accounting to meet operation standards and compliance requirements.

Administrative Management

- Administrative management is crucial for operational security.
- Personnel issues such as separation of duties and job rotation are key elements.
- **Separation of Duties**
  - Ensures no single person has control over all aspects of a high-risk task.
  - System administrators and users have distinct roles and permissions.
- **Job Rotation**
  - Multiple people learn the tasks of a position, providing redundancy.
  - Helps detect fraud as employees familiar with each other's roles can spot irregularities.
- **Least Privilege and Need to Know**
  - Users only get access necessary for their roles, reducing risk.
  - Access control enforced by identity management software.

- **Security Modes of Operation**
  - Systems operate based on data sensitivity, user clearance, and authorized actions.
  - Security modes are defined based on these factors.
- **Mandatory Vacations**
  - Help uncover fraudulent activities like salami attacks.
  - Another employee may detect irregularities during the absence of the regular employee.

Security and Network Personnel

- The security administrator should not report to the network administrator to avoid conflicts of interest.
- Security administrators are responsible for implementing and maintaining security measures and policies.

Accountability

- User access must be controlled and monitored for auditing and accountability.
- Privileged accounts need management to prevent authorization creep.
- **Auditing**
  - Regular auditing and review of logs are necessary to detect unauthorized access or excessive privileges.
  - Logs should be monitored to identify security shifts and potential issues.

Clipping Levels

- Thresholds for acceptable error rates can be set, with excesses triggering reviews.
- Intrusion Detection Systems (IDS) often monitor these activities due to the volume of data.
- **Inconspicuous Security Controls**
  - Security controls should be subtle to allow users to work efficiently and prevent attackers from easily circumventing them.

Physical Security

- Layered approach to security is crucial for effective defense against intrusions.
- Diversity of controls is important; each entry should have unique keys or authentication.

Facility Access Control

- Physical access controls identify and allow authorized individuals while keeping others out.
- Access control points should be identified and protected; different entrances for personnel, deliveries, and sensitive areas.
- Personnel within sensitive areas serve as strong security controls and need to be trained to detect and report suspicious behavior.
- **Locks**
  - Locks are basic but essential elements of security, acting as delaying devices.
  - They should not be the sole security measure due to risks of keys being lost, copied, or locks being picked.
  - Various types of locks exist, including padlocks, preset locks, programmable locks, and cipher locks.
- **Mechanical Locks**
  - Warded and tumbler locks are two main types of mechanical locks.

- Warded locks are basic and easy to pick, while tumbler locks have more security features.
- Three types of tumbler locks are pin tumbler, wafer tumbler, and lever tumbler.
- **Electronic Locks and Cipher Locks**
  - Electronic combination locks use a keypad for entry instead of a key.
  - Cipher locks offer higher security by allowing programmable combinations and are often keyless.
  - Functionalities include door delay, key override, master keying, and hostage alarms.
- **Device Locks**
  - Device locks are necessary to prevent hardware theft and include cable locks, slot locks, and port controls.
- **Administrative Responsibilities**
  - Proper management of locks, keys, and combinations is essential.

- **Circumventing Locks**
  - Lock picking tools and techniques, like tension wrenches and lock bumping, can be used to open locks without keys.
  - Locks are available in various grades for different security levels.

Personnel Access Controls
- Proper identification is critical for verifying access rights, using biometrics, smart cards, or photo IDs.

External Boundary Protection Mechanisms
- Include access control, physical barriers, intrusion detection, assessment, response, and deterrents.
- Fencing, lighting, gates, and surveillance devices are part of perimeter security.
- **Fencing**
  - Fencing is both a psychological deterrent and physical barrier, and should be well-maintained and appropriate for the threat level.
  - Different heights and types of fencing offer varying levels of security.
- **Lighting**
  - Proper lighting is critical for security and safety, with no unlit areas.
  - Types of lighting include continuous lighting, standby lighting, and responsive area illumination.
  - Lighting controls should be protected and centralized.
- **Surveillance Devices**
  - Closed-Circuit TV (CCTV) systems are common and should be tailored to the environment and security needs.
  - CCTVs use cameras, transmitters, receivers, recording systems, and monitors.
  - Various lenses and mounting options offer different fields of view and depth of field.

Intrusion Detection Systems (IDS)
- IDSs detect unauthorized entries and sound alarms.
- They can monitor changes in light, sound, motion, and electrical circuits.
- Different types of detectors include electromechanical and volumetric systems.

Patrol Force and Guards
- Security guards are flexible and responsive security mechanisms but can be costly.
- They may have specific responsibilities, like monitoring IDSs, checking credentials, and securing areas.

Dogs
- Dogs can be an effective supplementary security mechanism.

Auditing Physical Access
- Physical access control systems produce logs that track access attempts.
- Logs should be reviewed regularly to ensure security.

Internal Security Controls
- Include work area separation, personnel badging, visitor management, and roving guards.
- Training and clear protocols are essential for personnel to respond to incidents effectively.

Secure Resource Provisioning
- In technology, it broadly refers to providing new information services to users.
- Crucial to ensure services are secure and accessed securely, adhering to authorizations and the least privilege principle.

Asset Inventory
- Essential to know what assets (hardware and software) are being defended.
- Hardware tracking challenges include supply chain security, detecting unauthorized devices, and ensuring legitimate acquisition.
- Software tracking is vital to avoid liability issues and security risks from unlicensed or pirated software.
- Best practices include application whitelisting, using Gold Masters, enforcing least privilege, and automated scanning.

Asset Management
- A cyclical process consisting of business case, acquisition, Operation and Maintenance (O&M), and retirement phases.
- Change management board oversees asset acquisition to ensure compatibility and minimal risk introduction.
- Operation phase configures assets for functionality, non-interference, and security; configurations may change over time.
- **Media Management**
  - Media stores information and includes hard drives, optical discs, tapes, and paper.
  - Security considerations for media should be integrated into the asset management phases.
- **Hardware and Software Asset Management**
  - Hardware asset management involves tracking and life-cycle management, often aided by IT asset

management systems.
  - Software asset management focuses on compliance with licensing agreements and security against unauthorized distributions.

Configuration Management
- Establishes and maintains consistent system baselines.
- Policies determine change procedures and approvals and documentation practices.
- Change management is a business process, whereas configuration management is more operational and technical.
- **Change Control Process**
  - Structured process involving request, approval, documentation, testing, implementation, and reporting of changes.

Trusted Recovery
- Systems should recover securely from crashes without compromising security.
- Recovery processes, such as system reboot, emergency restart, and cold start, aim to achieve a secure, stable state.

Input and Output Controls
- Input should be validated to prevent errors and malicious data entry.
- Transactions should be atomic, timestamped, and secure.
- Output must be securely delivered and properly labeled with appropriate access controls.

System Hardening
- Physical, administrative, and technical controls are needed to secure systems.
- Develop standard hardened images (Gold Masters) for workstations to ensure secure configurations.

- **Licensing Issues**
  -It is an ethical obligation to use legitimately purchased software.
  - Operations or configuration management departments track software installations and licenses to prevent piracy

Remote Access Security
- Enables business continuity but introduces risks such as authentication challenges and the potential for compromised client devices.
- Secure remote administration includes VPNs, encryption, strong authentication, and local administration for critical systems.

Provisioning Cloud Assets
- Varies by service type (IaaS, PaaS, and SaaS) and organizational impact.

VERSAtile Reads

- Provisioning should be controlled to allow authorized users to access properly configured applications and services rapidly.
- **Secure Resource Provisioning and Failure Management**
  - Availability is a key component of security, alongside integrity and confidentiality.
  - Effective backup and redundant systems are essential to maintain productivity during system failures.

Network and Resource Availability

- Proper maintenance, including cable checks and updates, ensures network and resource availability.
- Redundant hardware, fault-tolerant technologies, and solid operational procedures are crucial for high availability.
- **Service Level Agreements (SLAs)**
  - SLAs determine the appropriate availability technology and help businesses understand the value of their information.

Mean Time Between Failures (MTBF)

- MTBF measures the average operational time between failures.
- MTTR (Mean Time to Repair) is the average time taken to restore a failed system or component to its normal functioning state.

Mean Time to Repair (MTTR)

- MTTR measures the time to fix or replace a failed device.
- Organizations monitor this metric to manage device maintenance and replacements.

Single Points of Failure

- Critical devices like firewalls and routers can be single points of failure.
- Protection against risk includes maintenance, backups, redundancy, and fault tolerance.
- **More components can mean less reliability.**
  - Adding more components can increase the chance of failure; redundancy and backups are necessary for critical data.
- **Redundant Array of Independent Disks (RAID)**
  - RAID technology provides redundancy and performance improvement by combining multiple disks into logical arrays.
- **DASD (Direct Access Storage Device) and MAID (Massive Array of Inactive Disks)**
  - DASD provides prompt access to any point on a storage device and they reduce energy consumption by powering down inactive disks.
- **RAIT (Redundant Array of Independent Tapes)**
  - Similar to RAID but uses tape drives;
  - suitable for large storage applications requiring cost-efficiency and reliability.
- **Storage Area Networks (SANs)**
  - SANs link numerous storage devices with high-speed private networks, offering redundancy, fault tolerance, and efficient backups.

- **Clustering and Grid Computing**
  - Clustering provides fault tolerance and load balancing with servers working in unison.
  - Grid computing uses spare processing power across loosely coupled systems for large-scale computations.

Backups
- Regular backups are vital for data restoration, Hardware Security Module (HSM)

- Manages storage by keeping frequently accessed files on faster media.

Contingency Planning
- Detailed procedures are required for dealing with incidents to keep critical systems available.
- Plans should be regularly tested and updated to match the changing IT environment.
- **Summary of Availability Technologies**
  - Technologies like redundant servers, RAID, SANs, clustering, and backups improve resource availability.
- **Understanding the Risk:**
  - Focus on mitigating the most dangerous risks to an acceptable level.
  - Allocate resources effectively by prioritizing risks that concern senior leaders.
- **Using the Right Controls:**
  - Match controls to risks using a many-to-many relationship.
  - Multiple controls for risk can provide resiliency, but efficiency may suffer.
- **Using Controls Correctly:**
  - Proper placement and configuration are crucial for tool effectiveness

Preventing and Detecting
- Essential for maintaining accurate knowledge of network configurations.
- Prevents unauthorized changes that could introduce risks.
- **Assessing Operations:**
  - Regular reviews of the defensive plan against current threats and risks.
  - Testing controls to ensure proper risk mitigation.

Continuous Monitoring
- Ongoing verification of security controls' effectiveness.
- Assesses if controls are still appropriate and effective against evolving threats.

Firewalls
- No longer universally used as stand-alone; integrated into broader security solutions.
- Placement and rule enforcement are vital for effectiveness.

Intrusion Detection Systems (IDS) and Intrusion Prevention Systems (IPS)
- Important to place sensors strategically within the network.
- Reducing false positives and negatives through careful configuration and baselining.

Whitelisting and Blacklisting
- Whitelists provide full knowledge of acceptable resources, while blacklists are used when not all resources can be known.
- Blacklists will always be incomplete due to the dynamic nature of the internet.

Antimalware
- Effective against known malware, but can be bypassed by new or modified threats.

Vulnerability Management
- Identifying and addressing software, process, and human vulnerabilities.
- Involves scanning, red team exercises, and social engineering assessments.

Patch Management
- Identifying, installing, and verifying patches for systems.
- **Reverse Engineering Patches**:
  - Attackers may use reverse engineering of patches to exploit vulnerabilities during update delays.

Sandboxing
- Isolating code execution to prevent security violations.

Honeypots and Honeynets
- Used to attract and observe attackers for threat intelligence.

Egress Monitoring
- Monitoring outbound network traffic to prevent data leaks and unauthorized communications.

Security Information and Event Management (SIEM)
- Aggregates and analyzes security information and events for better threat visibility.

Outsourced Services managed security service provider (MSSP)
- Managed Security Service Providers Managed Security Service Providers (MSSP) offer various security services.
- Useful for organizations lacking in-house security expertise.
- Due diligence is required when selecting an Managed Security Service Provider (MSSP). Due diligence is necessary when selecting a Managed Security Service Provider (MSSP) to ensure alignment with security needs, expertise, and reliability.

The Incident Management Process
- Involves identifying, analyzing, correcting, and preventing future occurrences of security events.

- (ISC)² outlines seven phases: detect, respond, mitigate, report, recover, remediate, and earn.
- Events are observable occurrences; incidents are events that negatively impact security.
- Companies should establish incident response policies and teams.
- **Incident Management**
  - Includes proactive measures for detection and reactive measures for proper handling.
  - A holistic incident management program ensures all incidents are detected and addressed.
  - Three types of response teams: virtual, permanent, and hybrid.
  - Teams need access to resources such as outside agencies, role outlines, contact lists, forensic experts, evidence preservation steps, and reporting guidelines.
- **The Cyber Kill Chain**
  - A seven-stage intrusion model: reconnaissance, weaponization, delivery, exploitation, installation, command and control, and actions on the objective.
  - Early detection is crucial for preventing adversaries from achieving their objectives.

Detection
- Recognizing a problem through sensors or reports is challenging due to sophisticated adversaries and false positives.

Response
- Understanding the adversary's objectives is key to an appropriate response.
- Response requires data gathering and analysis to determine the incident's root cause and extent.
- The response team must be skilled and knowledgeable about affected systems and configurations.

Mitigation
- Aim to prevent further damage and contain the incident.
- Strategies include system isolation, network segmentation, and firewall rule adjustments.
- Use of honeynets or honeypots can contain attackers but may introduce legal issues.

Reporting
- Ongoing documentation is vital for legal and investigative purposes.
- NIST suggests reporting incident summaries, indicators, actions taken, impact assessments, and next steps.

Recovery
- Returning systems to a known-good state involves evidence capture and system restoration from backups.
- Rebuilt systems ensure removal of all traces of malicious activity.

Remediation
- Permanent fixes and additional controls are implemented to prevent recurrence of the incident.
- Identifying Indicators of Attack (IOA) and compromise (IOC) assists in future real-time detection and security.

- **Part of the Incident Response Process**
    - Post-incident review to analyze what happened and identify improvements.
    - Formal briefing processes help in collecting performance metrics for continual improvement.

Investigations

- Treat all incidents as potential crime scenes to account for possible malicious activities.
- Understand legal requirements, chain of custody, admissible evidence, and incident response.
- Investigations encompass people, networks, systems, laws, management stance, and investigator skills.
- **Cops or No Cops?**
    - Management decides if law enforcement is involved.
    - Law enforcement brings investigative capabilities but may lead to loss of control over investigation and public disclosure.

Computer Forensics and Proper Collection of Evidence

- Forensics combines computer science, IT, engineering, and law.
- Requires specialized techniques for electronic data recovery and analysis.
- Evidence must be collected quickly and in order of volatility.
- Create documented sound system images for analysis to preserve original evidence.

Motive Opportunity and Means (MOM)

- Helps determine suspects in crimes by assessing internal/external conditions.
- Opportunity arises from vulnerabilities, which means it relates to the abilities required for the crime.

Computer Criminal Behavior

- Computer criminals have a Modus Operandi (MO) that can help identify them.
- Profiling provides insight into the attacker's thought processes.

Incident Investigators

- Skilled in noticing suspicious activities and analyzing forensic evidence.
- Must understand forensic procedures and evidence collection.
- **Different Types of Assessments an Investigator Can Perform**:
    - Network analysis, media analysis, software analysis, hardware/embedded device analysis.

Types of Investigations

- Administrative, criminal, civil, and regulatory, each with different focuses and implications.

The Forensic Investigation Process

- Follows phases of identification, preservation, collection, examination, analysis, presentation, and decision.
- Involves creating bit-level copies of evidence for analysis.

- **Controlling the Crime Scene**:
  - Limit access, document presence, and protect from contamination.
  - Maintain a chain of custody for evidence.
- **Forensics Field Kits**:
  - Include documentation tools, disassembly tools, and packaging supplies.

What Is Admissible in Court?

- Computer logs used as evidence in court must be collected in the regular course of business.
- The Business Records Exception rule allows admission of records made in the regular course of business.
- Evidence must be relevant, complete, sufficient, and reliable to be legally permissible in court.

Surveillance, Search, and Seizure

- Includes physical and computer surveillance.
- Search and seizure must follow legal procedures and protect against unlawful practices.
- **Evidence Chain of Custody**:
  - Essential to maintain integrity and admissibility in court.
  - Includes collection, storage, presentation, and return or destruction of evidence.
- **Distinguishing Between Enticement and Entrapment**:
  - Enticement is legal, while entrapment is neither legal nor ethical.
  - Honeypots can be used to entice and monitor attackers without crossing into entrapment.

Disaster Recovery (DR)

- DR is mainly under the purview of information systems operations and security.
- **Maximum Tolerable Downtime (MTD)**:
  - Provides a deadline for restoring services to avoid catastrophic business failure.
  - MTD alone is insufficient.
- **Key Metrics in DR**:
  - **Recovery Time Objective (RTO):** Maximum time to restore a business process after a disaster.
  - **Work Recovery Time (WRT):** Time to restore data and test processes after RTO is met.
  - **Recovery Point Objective (RPO):** Acceptable amount of data loss measured in time.
- **Business Impact Analysis (BIA)**:
  - Determines criticality values for business functions and data.
  - Helps derive MTD, RTO, and RPO values for planning recovery solutions.
- **Recovery Solutions**:
  - Should be based on the type of data and processing criticality.
  - Solutions range from manual processes to high availability data replication.
  - The right tactics and technologies should assure MTD values are met.
- **Preventive Measures vs. Recovery Strategies**:
  - Preventive mechanisms aim to reduce disaster impact.
  - Recovery strategies are processes to rescue the company post-disaster.

Business Process Recovery

- Detailed understanding of critical business processes is necessary.

- Workflow documents should outline roles, resources, and steps for recovery.

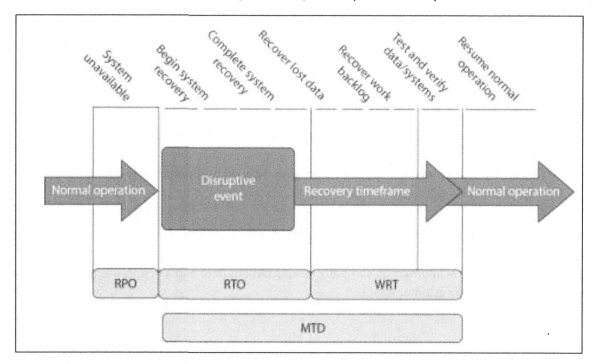

Recovery Site Strategies
- Options include redundant sites, hot/warm/cold sites, reciprocal agreements, and service bureaus.
- Important considerations include recovery time, priority, costs, and reliability of the facility.

Supply and Technology Recovery
- A comprehensive approach is needed, encompassing technology, processes, and people.
- Regular testing and updates are essential to validate and improve recovery capabilities.

End-User Environment
- BCP teams must understand the current operational and technical environment to replicate critical pieces for end users post-disaster.
- Establish a notification tree structure for managers to disseminate information to end users effectively.
- Prioritize critical functions and departments to bring back online in stages, considering user requirements and potential manual workarounds for automated tasks.

Availability
- Detailed documentation is crucial for successful recovery.
- High Availability (HA) involves technologies and processes to ensure system readiness and uptime.

Backup Storage Strategies
- Multiple factors must be evaluated, like access times, environmental hazards, and security measures.

Liability and it is Ramifications

- Organizations must develop approaches for liability and responsibility alongside preventive, detective, and corrective measures.
- Companies are responsible for implementing fire safety measures and backing up important data to avoid liability in case of a fire.
- Due care involves acting responsibly and ensuring reasonable measures are taken to prevent and mitigate damage from security breaches.
- Due diligence is about investigating vulnerabilities and risks to make informed decisions and protect the company from potential harm.
- Company's security policies and practices must align with industry best practices to avoid negligence.

Liability Scenarios

- Companies that fail to protect sensitive data or implement necessary security measures can be held liable for negligence.
- Examples include a medical information company leaking patient data and a financial institution failing to secure online banking, leading to customer losses.

Third-Party Risk

- Organizations must assess third-party security measures as they are still liable for their own data, even if it resides on another company's network.
- Contracts with third parties should address security considerations to mitigate downstream liability.

Contractual Agreements

- Security issues must be integrated into various contracts, such as outsourcing and software licensing agreements.
- Contracts should cover regulatory, legal, and security requirements and be reviewed periodically for relevance and protection levels.

Procurement and Vendor Processes

- Security requirements are included in the procurement process and RFPs.
- Vendor management involves monitoring relationships and ensuring vendors meet security and performance standards.
- Organizations are responsible for their own risk and must have processes to assess and monitor vendor compliance and performance.

Insurance

- Business Impact Analysis (BIA) helps identify threats that can't be prevented.
- Insurance decisions should be based on threat probability and potential loss identified during BIA.
- **Role of the BCP Team:**
  - Work with management to review current coverage.

VERSAtile Reads

- Explore insurance options and understand their limits.
- Ensure coverage fills gaps not protected by preventive measures.
- **Purpose of Insurance:**
  - To protect against unexpected events, similar to how individuals use medical insurance for health issues.
- **Premium Determination for Companies:**
  - Factors like security programs, IDS, antivirus, and firewalls affect insurance premiums.
- **Types of Business Insurance:**
  - Cyber insurance covers losses from cyber threats like malware, hacking, and privacy lawsuits.
  - Business interruption insurance compensates for expenses and lost earnings during downtime.
  - Accounts receivable insurance covers losses when a company can't collect on its receivables.
- **Annual Review of Insurance:**
  - Necessary to adjust for changing threat levels and new ventures.
- **Limitations and Responsibilities:**
  - Insurance has limitations; due care is essential.
  - Companies must understand the fine print and fulfill obligations to ensure coverage in the event of a disaster.

Implementing Disaster Recovery

- Disaster recovery begins with anticipating threats and setting goals for business continuity.
- Goals ensure a clear end-point for recovery efforts and guide resource allocation.
- Responsibility, authority, and priorities must be clearly defined for effective recovery.
- Implementation and testing of plans are crucial; drills should be done annually.

Personnel

- Disaster Recovery (DR) coordinator defines necessary teams: damage assessment, recovery, relocation, restoration, salvage and security.
- Team members are selected based on skills and knowledge.
- Team leaders coordinate and ensure objectives are met and communicate progress.

Assessment

- A damage assessment team or role is necessary post-disaster.
- Assessment procedures include determining the cause, potential for further damage, and affected areas.
- Activation criteria for the Business Continuity Plan (BCP) are established based on this assessment.

Restoration

- Post-assessment, teams are deployed to restore operations.
- Critical functions are prioritized for restoration.
- Templates guide teams through necessary steps and documentation.

Communications

- An emergency communication strategy is part of the DR plan.
- Multiple formats and locations for the DR plan are necessary to ensure accessibility.

- Call trees, group messages, and independent communication platforms are recommended for coordination.
- Primary, Alternate, Contingency, and Emergency (PACE) communication plans are used for structured communication strategy.

Training
- Training validates the DR plan's effectiveness and familiarizes the team with their roles.
- Regular training aims to establish a routine.
- Shows due diligence, potentially reducing liability in the event of a disaster.

Personal Safety Concerns
The safety of employees, visitors, and clients in both physical and virtual spaces is a top priority.

Emergency Management
- Occupant Emergency Plans (OEPs) guide personnel on actions to take during emergencies.
- Physical access controls must balance security with emergency exit strategies.
- Emergency responder access and fail-safe devices are crucial for safety during power outages.

Duress
- Involves threats to force someone to act against their will.
- Countermeasures include hidden panic buttons and duress codes for alarms and systems.
- Duress codes can be discreet signals, such as verbal cues or alternate login credentials.

Travel
- Employee safety during travel requires assessing the destination's threat landscape.
- Utilize government travel advisories and embassy/consulate contact information.

Training
- Staff must be trained and regularly updated on personal safety measures, emergency procedures, and security protocols.

Mind Map

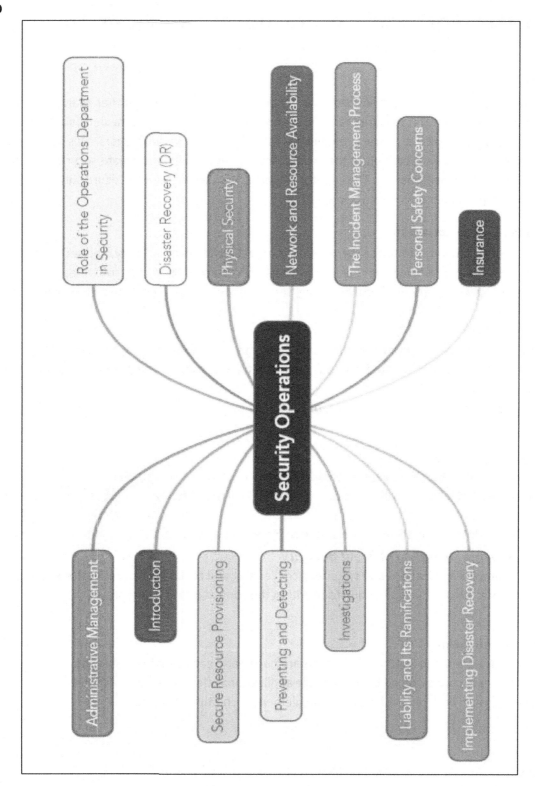

Chapter 09: Software Development Security

Introduction

Effective software development should prioritize both functionality and security. Rather than treating security as an afterthought, it is essential to integrate security controls seamlessly into each phase of the development life-cycle. Security should be a fundamental part of the product, providing protection across various layers. This approach is superior to adding a separate front end or wrapper, which may compromise functionality and create security vulnerabilities during integration into a production environment. The chapter will explore the intricacies of secure software development and the consequences of neglecting proper security integration.

Building Good Code Quality

- Quality in software means fitness for purpose, ensuring reliability, data integrity, and security.
- Functionality is often prioritized over quality, but quality is essential for secure software.
- Quality assurance entails comprehensive testing, such as code reviews, interface testing, and misuse case testing.
- **Software Controls**:
  - Controls are necessary for system security and come in various forms (input, encryption, logic, etc.).
  - The type of controls implemented depends on the software's purpose, data processing, and operating environment.
  - Controls should be preventive, detective, or corrective and developed with potential risks in mind.

Where Do We Place Security?

- Historically, security focused on perimeter defenses due to software vulnerabilities.
- Causes include a lack of security focus in development, time-to-market pressures, and acceptance of software flaws.
- Shifting towards integrating security into software from the development stage is necessary for this change.

Different Environments Demand Different Security

- Integrating complex applications and systems is challenging and requires comprehensive security measures.
- Security needs to be planned and understood within the context of the environment.

Environment vs. Application

- Both operating system and application controls are necessary, each with its limitations.
- Operating systems provide broad controls, while applications offer specific protections.
- The key is to ensure both types of controls complement each other effectively.

Functionality vs. Security

- Balancing functionality and security is challenging; traditionally, functionality wins.
- Security considerations can add complexity and reduce marketability but are necessary for a secure product.

Implementation and Default Issues
- Many systems come with insecure default configurations, requiring post-installation security setup.
- Implementation errors and misconfigurations are common security issues.
- Patch management is critical but often neglected, leaving systems vulnerable.
- **Conclusion**:
  - The best approach to security is preventive, integrating it into the software during development.
  - This proactive stance reduces the need for reactive measures, such as patches, after deployment.

Software Development Life-Cycle (SDLC)
- Implementing repeatable and predictable processes for functionality, cost, quality, and schedule.
- Phases: requirements gathering, design, development, testing, operations, and maintenance.

Project Management
- Keeps the project on track and allocates resources.
- Integrates a security plan from the beginning for thorough consideration in each phase.
- References standards, previous documents, and policies for guidance.

Requirements Gathering Phase
- Understand the project's need and scope.
- Examines software's requirements, functionalities, restrictions, and market demand.
- Security tasks include security requirements, security and privacy risk assessments, and risk-level acceptance determination.

Design Phase
- Translates requirements into product design.
- Uses informational, functional, and behavioral models for requirements.
- Security tasks include attack surface analysis and threat modeling.

Development Phase
- Programmers write code to meet specifications.
- Use of Computer-Aided Software Engineering (CASE) tools to automate coding and testing.
- Focus on secure coding practices to prevent common vulnerabilities.
- **Static Analysis**
  - Analyzing code without executing it to identify defects or policy violations.
  - Performed before program compilation.

Testing Phase
- Begin testing as soon as possible with unit testing.
- Utilizes fuzzers for malformed data testing and dynamic analysis for real-time program evaluation.

- Relays issues found to the development team for fixes.

- Different testing types include unit, integration, acceptance, and regression testing.

Operations and Maintenance Phase
- Release and implement software in production environments.
- Address newly discovered problems and add new features over time.
- Verification ensures product meets specifications, validation ensures it solves the intended problem.
- Develop patches and updates for security vulnerabilities discovered post-release.
- **SDLC and Security**
  - Security integrated into every phase of SDLC.
  - Important to perform security risk assessments, threat modeling, attack surface analysis, and static and dynamic analysis.
  - Regular updates and maintenance to address new security threats and vulnerabilities.

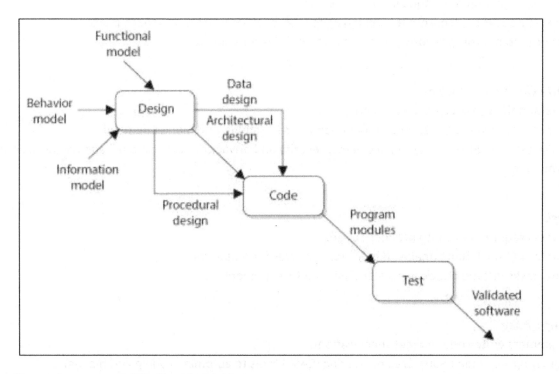

Software Development Methodologies
- Multiple methodologies exist, each with unique characteristics, advantages, disadvantages, and suitability for different project types.
- A Real-world application often involves customizing a base methodology to fit an organization's specific needs.

Waterfall Methodology
- Linear-sequential life-cycle approach.
- Each phase must be completed before the next begins, with reviews at the end of each phase.

- Difficult to integrate changes once the project has started, not ideal for complex projects.

V-Shaped Methodology
- Similar to waterfall but includes testing at each development phase.
- Still rigid and difficult to adapt to changes, better suited for projects with well-understood requirements.

Prototyping
- Develops a model or sample of the software to test solutions before full-scale development.
- Includes rapid, evolutionary, and operational prototypes, with each serving different purposes in the development process.

Incremental Methodology
- Multiple "mini-waterfall" cycles that produce operational products at each phase.
- Early delivery of a working version, flexibility for changes, and better risk management.

Spiral Methodology
- An iterative approach focusing on risk analysis at each phase.
- Involves customers for feedback and improves the product through multiple iterations, suitable for complex and fluid projects.

Rapid Application Development (RAD)
- Focuses on rapid prototyping over extensive planning.
- Allows for fast development with customer involvement, addressing changing requirements quickly.

Agile Methodologies
- Encourages incremental, iterative development with team collaboration and continuous feedback.
- Emphasizes adaptability and customer involvement over strict process adherence.
- **Scrum**
  - Widely adopted Agile framework for projects of any size.
  - Iterative development with customer input at the end of each sprint.
- **Extreme Programming (XP)**
  - Emphasizes continuous code review through pair programming.
  - Uses test-driven development with unit tests written before the code.
- **Kanban**
  - Visual task tracking to prioritize tasks and deliver features on time.
- **Review of Development Methodologies**
  - Summarizes each methodology's key points, including their rigidity, flexibility, customer involvement, and iterative nature.
- **Other Methodologies**
  - Includes exploratory, Joint Application Development (JAD), reuse, and cleanroom methodologies, each serving

VERSAtile Reads

specific development needs.

Integrated Product Team (IPT)
- A multidisciplinary team approach that includes various stakeholders.

DevOps
- Integrates development, IT, and QA staff into projects for efficient releases.
- Focuses on organizational culture change, improving security, trust, job satisfaction, and reducing friction between teams.

Capability Maturity Model Integration (CMMI)
- A set of comprehensive guidelines for software product development.
- Covers various phases of the software development life-cycle.
- Helps evaluate and improve security engineering practices.
- Used by vendors for process improvement and by customers for vendor evaluation.
- **The Five Maturity Levels of CMMI**
  - **Initial**: Processes are ad hoc and unmanaged; success relies on individual effort.
  - **Repeatable**: Formal management with change control and quality assurance exists.
  - **Defined**: Processes are well-documented and standardized across projects.
  - **Managed**: Quantitative data is collected and analyzed for process improvement.
  - **Optimizing**: Continuous process improvement is planned and budgeted.
- **Application of CMMI**
  - Software vendors often seek CMMI evaluation for credibility and customer confidence.
  - A vendor using prototyping may only achieve Level 1 if practices are inconsistent.
  - A vendor consistently using Agile SDLC could achieve a higher CMMI level.
- **Capability Maturity Models (CMMs)**
  - CMMs identify maturity levels and improvement steps for various processes.
  - Developed by industry experts, government, and Carnegie Mellon's Software Engineering Institute.
  - CMMI replaces CMM in software engineering but CMM may still be referenced.
- **Latest CMMI Updates**
  - CMMI is continually updated; latest version is available at the SEI website.
- **Other Maturity Models**
  - **DevOps Maturity Model**: Focuses on integrating development and operations teams.
  - **Open-source Maturity Model (OSMM)**: Measures effectiveness in open-source software processes.
  - **Software Product Management Maturity Model**: Addresses business aspects of software product development.

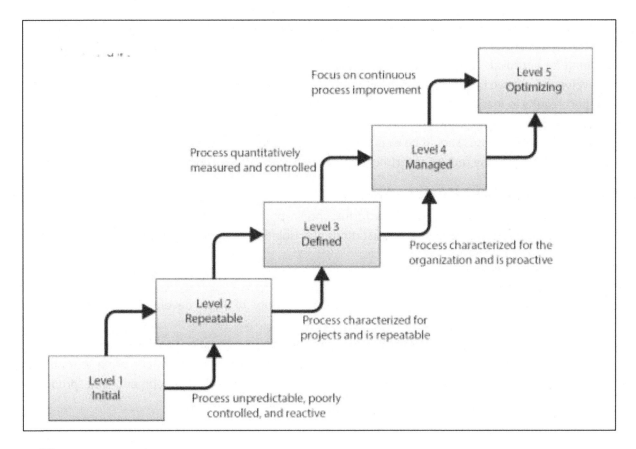

Change Management

- Focus on managing inevitable changes to prevent disruption.
- Changes can arise during development or in production due to various reasons.
- Changes should be carefully analyzed, approved, and integrated without harming original functionality.
- Change management considers technical, resource, project life-cycle, and organizational aspects.

Change Control

- Process of controlling and documenting changes throughout a system's life-cycle.
- Changes must be approved, documented, and tested, with possible retesting.
- Programmers should alter the test code, not the production code.
- A change management process should be established early in the project to set expectations.
- **Importance of Change Control**
  - Prevents customers from requesting endless changes without cost, avoiding scope creep.
  - Ensures organization, standard procedures, and expected results.
  - Helps manage late-stage development changes effectively.
- **Risks of Poor Change Control**
  - Uncoordinated changes can lead to incompatibilities and software failure.
  - The absence of approval for changes can jeopardize jobs and management accountability.
- **Change Control Process Steps**
  1. Formally request a change.

2. Analyze the request, develop an implementation strategy, calculate costs, and review security.

3. Record the change request.

4. Submit for approval.

5. Develop the change by recode, test, quality control, and version changes.

6. Report results to management.

- **System Audits and Change Control**
  - Change control processes should be evaluated during system audits to catch overlooked issues.
  - Significant changes may require recertification and reaccreditation of the system.

Security of Development Environments

- Importance of security for development platforms, code repositories, and software configurations.
- Challenges include securing developer workstations and isolating development from production environments.

Security of Development Platforms

- Secure development platforms involve ensuring the security of both development endpoints and testing environments.
- Enforce change management practices to prevent unauthorized modifications to developers' workstations.
- Isolate development clients and servers from production environments, potentially using VPNs or VLANs, and involve operations staff in provisioning to maintain separation of development and production code.

Security of Code Repositories

- Code repositories, which host source code, must be protected as they contain intellectual property.
- An isolated (air-gapped) network is the most secure way to manage code repositories.
- Secure Shell (SSH) with Public Key Infrastructure (PKI) can secure repositories on an intranet.
- Web-based repository service providers are an option for organizations with limited resources.

Software Configuration Management (SCM)

- Manage and track changes during software development.
- They provide version control, concurrency management, and synchronization.
- Ensures software integrity and traceability through the development life-cycle.
- **Software Escrow**
  - Involves a third-party holding source code to protect a customer if the vendor fails.
  - It ensures customers can maintain and update software if the vendor goes out of business.
  - Source code is often the vendor's intellectual property, and customers typically receive compiled code.
  - The source code may be provided for an additional fee for sensitive applications.

Secure Coding

- Developing software without defects to prevent exploitation by adversaries.
- Aim for defect-free software, a standard for all projects.

Source Code Vulnerabilities

- Open Web Application Security Project (OWASP) focuses on web security issues.
- Provides tools, guidelines, testing procedures, and code review steps.
- Known for OWASP Top 10 list of web application security risks (2017 version provided).
- **OWASP Top 10 (2017)**
    - A1: Injection
    - A2: Broken Authentication
    - A3: Sensitive Data Exposure
    - A4: XML External Entities
    - A5: Broken Access Control
    - A6: Security Misconfiguration
    - A7: Cross-Site Scripting (XSS)
    - A8: Insecure Deserialization
    - A9: Using Components with Known Vulnerabilities
    - A10: Insufficient Logging & Monitoring
    - Common vulnerabilities in web applications

Secure Coding Practices

- Initially developed in an ad hoc manner until the need for structured practices was recognized.
- Carnegie Mellon University's Software Engineering Institute (SEI) provides secure coding standards.
- **SEI's Top 10 Secure Coding Practices**
    1. Validate inputs - never trust inputs.
    2. Heed compiler warnings.
    3. Architect and design for security policies.
    4. Keep code simple - conduct regular code reviews.
    5. Default deny - unless explicitly required to allow requests.
    6. Adhere to the principle of least privilege.
    7. Sanitize data sent to other systems.
    8. Practice defense in depth.
    9. Use effective quality assurance techniques.
    10. Adopt a secure coding standard.
- **ISO/IEC Standards**
    - ISO/IEC 27034 provides secure coding guidance.
    - Part of the ISO/IEC 27000 series, aligning development processes with the ISMS model.
    - Covers various aspects including an overview, organization framework, management processes, and assurance prediction.

Programming Languages and Concepts

- Programming has evolved through generations, from machine language to natural language.
- Machine language is binary and processor-specific.
- Assembly language uses mnemonics and requires knowledge of computer architecture.
- High-level languages allow abstraction from low-level system intricacies.

- Fourth-generation languages reduce the amount of coding needed.
- Fifth-generation languages aim to solve problems using AI and eliminate the need for traditional programming.
- **Language Levels:**
  - Higher-level languages provide more abstraction, hiding complex system details.
  - Allows Programmers to focus on application functionality rather than system operations.

Assemblers, Compilers, and Interpreters
- Assemblers transform assembly language into machine code.
- Compilers convert high-level language to an executable format for specific processors.
- Interpreters translate high-level code to machine-level code at runtime, improving portability.

Object-Oriented Concepts
- OOP uses classes and objects to model real-world entities and their interactions.
- Encapsulation hides the internal workings of an object, only exposing an APIs.
- Polymorphism allows objects to respond differently to the same input.
- Benefits include modularity, reusability, and easier maintenance.

Other Software Development Concepts
- Data modeling focuses on logical relationships and the correctness of data processing.
- Data structures represent the organization and association among data elements.
- Cohesion measures how focused a module's tasks are; high cohesion is preferred.
- Coupling indicates the degree of inter-module interaction; low coupling is desired.
- Complex structures can impact security, with simpler structures being more secure.

Application Programming Interfaces (APIs)
- APIs define how software components interact, promoting reuse and maintainability.
- Software libraries use APIs to provide commonly needed functionalities.
- Operating systems and computing frameworks often require the use of standard APIs.

Distributed Computing
- Applications often use a client/server model, with clients making requests and servers responding.
- Distributed object computing requires registering client and server components to manage communication.

Distributed Computing Environment (DCE)
- Developed by the Open Software Foundation, DCE is a client/server framework.
- Provides Remote Procedure Call (RPC), security, directory, time services, and distributed file support.
- DCE was a pioneering attempt at standardizing communication across heterogeneous systems.
- Time synchronization and directory services are key functionalities.
- DCE uses Universally Unique IDentifier (UUIDs) for identifying network components.

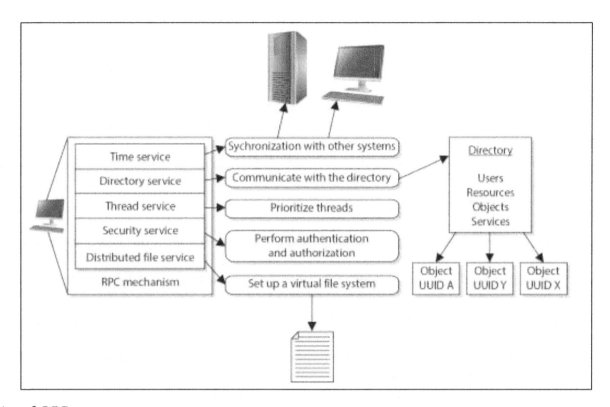

CORBA and ORBs

- CORBA, by OMG, is an open, object-oriented standard for software interoperability.
- It uses standard APIs and communication protocols for distributed applications.
- Object Request Brokers (ORBs) handle communications between components, enabling interactions in a distributed environment.

COM and DCOM

- Microsoft's COM allows inter-process communication within one system; DCOM extends this over a network.
- DCOM simplifies developer tasks by handling complex network communication processes.
- .NET framework largely replaces DCOM, providing a comprehensive library and virtual machine execution for Windows environments.
- **Object Linking and Embedding (OLE)**
  - Allows sharing of objects like graphics and spreadsheets within documents on a PC.
  - Uses COM as its foundation and has evolved into ActiveX for the web, which supports DCOM communication.

Java Platform, Enterprise Edition (Java EE)

- A framework for developing enterprise software with Java, focusing on large-scale, multi-tiered network applications.
- Offers APIs for essential services such as networking and security, and is based on CORBA for interprocess-communication.

Service-Oriented Architecture (SOA)

- SOA offers standardized access to services for various applications.
- Services are modular, autonomous, and loosely coupled, providing functionality that can be reused across applications.
- A service broker acts as a directory for available services, which are usually provided through web services using standards like Simple Object Access Protocol (SOAP) and Web Services Description Language (WSDL).
- **SOAP**
  - An XML-based protocol used in web services to encode and communicate messages between applications on different systems.
  - Utilizes standard web formats and is often firewall-friendly due to its use of HTTP.
- **Cloud Computing and SaaS**
  - Cloud computing offers computing resources as a service over the internet, including storage, processing, and software.
  - SaaS is a model of cloud computing where applications are centrally hosted and accessed via thin clients or browsers.
- **Security Considerations in Distributed Computing**
  - Ensuring secure communication between client and server components is complex and essential.
  - Security measures must include mutual authentication, cryptographic compatibility, data integrity, and potentially secure transmission channels.
  - Security needs to be integrated at every level, including inter-process communication.

Mobile Code

- It can be executed by a system after being transmitted across a network.
- It's used for legitimate purposes, like web browser applets for downloading content.

Java Applets

- Java is platform-independent, using bytecode run by a Java Virtual Machine (JVM).
- Applets run in web browsers and are limited by a sandbox for security.
- Despite security measures like garbage collection and memory management, some applets can breach security and access restricted resources.

ActiveX Controls

- ActiveX is a Microsoft technology for creating reusable programs in Windows.
- These controls can add functionality to websites but can also compromise system security.
- Initially not a security risk, but embedding in web pages introduced vulnerabilities.
- ActiveX controls have the same privilege level as the user, posing a security threat.
- They can download additional components without user authentication, facilitating worm spread.
- Security levels and authentication settings are configurable by users.
- Unlike Java applets, ActiveX controls are stored on the user's hard drive.
- ActiveX relies on Authenticode technology with digital certificates, but this does not guarantee security.
- Microsoft Edge no longer supports ActiveX.

Web Security

- The internet exposes businesses to a vast audience, requiring them to open ports for web traffic, which can be avenues for attacks.
- Web applications used for e-commerce are complex and come with security risks, especially for those unfamiliar with web development.
- Businesses face a dilemma between creating custom applications with potential security flaws or using off-the-shelf solutions with uncertain security measures.

Specific Threats for Web Environments

- Administrative interfaces present risks if not secured properly, such as remote management potentially allowing unauthorized access.
- Authentication and access control are essential but often rely on weak methods like passwords, which attackers can target.
- Input validation is critical to prevent attackers from manipulating web servers by sending malformed or malicious requests.
- Parameter validation ensures that application-received values are checked before being processed, preventing manipulations like session cookie tampering.
- Session management is challenged by managing numerous client connections, with unique session IDs being susceptible to theft or prediction.

Web Application Security Principles

- Websites are prime targets for attacks, making adherence to security principles crucial.
- Website architecture and user-generated input should be analyzed and sanitized to prevent exploitation.
- Employ encryption to secure data transmission and design systems to fail securely without revealing critical information.
- Balance security and functionality, avoiding overly tedious authentication that may be bypassed by users.
- Recognize that a website's security is only as strong as its weakest link, which could compromise an organization's data.

Database Management

- Databases hold valuable proprietary information for companies, often shrouded in secrecy except for administrators.
- Users access databases indirectly through client interfaces with restricted actions for data confidentiality, integrity, and availability.
- Increased risks due to internet connectivity, remote access, and external entity access to databases.
- Middleware connects customers to databases via a browser, adding complexity and new access methods.
- Role-based access control is used to ensure that only authorized roles can interact with the database, providing indirect access only.

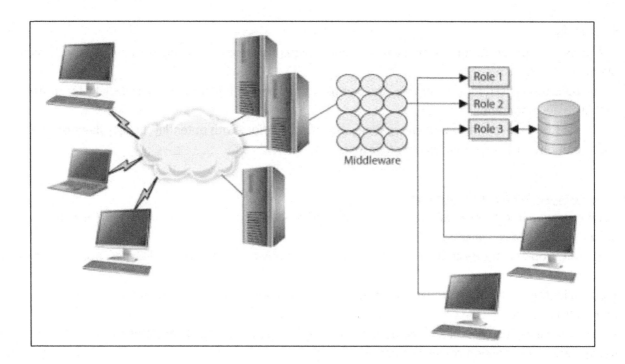

Database Management Software
- Manages data access, integrity, redundancy, and security.
- DBMS interfaces with programs, users, and the structured data within the database.
- Different data models cater to varying business and organizational needs, with features like consistency, backup ease, transaction persistence, recovery, data sharing, and security controls.

Database Models
- Various models include relational, hierarchical, network, object-oriented, and Object-relational.
- Relational model: widely used, organizes data in tables with primary keys linking data.
- Hierarchical model: tree structure with parent/child relationships, lacks flexibility, used for indexes and LDAP.
- Network model: allows multiple parent and child records creating a mesh-like structure for redundancy.
- Object-oriented model: handles dynamic data types and includes methods with objects for data processing.
- Object-relational model (ORD/ORDBMS): combines a relational database with object-oriented front end for data manipulation.

Database Programming Interfaces
- Open Database Connectivity (ODBC), Object Linking and Embedding Database (OLE DB), ActiveX Data Objects (ADO), and Java Database Connectivity (JDBC) are interfaces allowing applications to interact with databases.

Relational Database Components
- Databases have a Data Definition Language (DDL), Data Manipulation Language (DML), Data Control Language (DCL), and Query Language (QL) for structure, manipulation, control, and data access.

- A data dictionary centralizes data element definitions and relationships, holding schema objects and reference keys.

Database Security Issues

- Aggregation and inference are key security issues, where users combine lower-level data to infer higher-level sensitive information.
- Preventive measures include containerization, context-dependent access control, and techniques like cell suppression, partitioning, and noise insertion.
- **Database Views**
  - Database views control access to data based on user roles or security labels, using discretionary access control (DAC) or mandatory access control (MAC).
- **Polyinstantiation**
  - Allows multiple instances of a data item at different security levels to prevent lower-level users from accessing or modifying higher-level data.
- **Online Transaction Processing (OLTP)**
  - Manages real-time transaction processing, ensuring data integrity across clustered databases with features like process monitoring, rollback, commit, and the ACID test (Atomicity, Consistency, Isolation, Durability).

Data Warehousing and Data Mining

- Data warehousing consolidates data from multiple sources for analysis, while data mining extracts meaningful patterns and relationships.
- Knowledge Discovery in Databases (KDD) uses classification, probabilistic, and statistical methods for pattern identification.
- **Big Data**
  - Refers to large, complex, heterogeneous, and voluminous data sets not suited for traditional analysis, requiring specialized systems and approaches for exploitation.

Malicious Software (Malware)

- Threat actors range from lone hackers to nation-state operatives.
- Malware types include viruses, worms, Trojan horses, and logic bombs.
- Common infection methods like email, media sharing, downloads, and direct insertion by attackers.
- Combat strategies: cautious email handling, though not foolproof due to address book infections.
- Automated malware attacks can compromise thousands of systems simultaneously.
- **Increasing Sophistication of Malware**
  - Traditional detection methods are less effective; advanced malware can reside in RAM or execute drive-by downloads.
  - Malware often targets common software and devices, exploiting the digital storage and connectivity of sensitive data.

Viruses

- Viruses replicate by attaching themselves to files and require a host application.
- Types include macro virus, boot sector virus, stealth virus, polymorphic virus, multipart virus and script virus.

- Famous examples like ILOVEYOU and Melissa used email applications to spread.
- **Malware Components**
  - Common elements: insertion, avoidance, eradication, replication, trigger, and payload.

Worms
- Worms are self-replicating programs that do not require a host.
- Stuxnet is a notable example that targeted SCADA systems.

Rootkit
- Rootkits provide deep system access, including back-doors and credential capture.
- Difficult to detect, potentially requiring OS reinstallation for removal.

Spyware and Adware
- Spyware gathers sensitive information, often leading to identity theft.
- Adware generates revenue through targeted advertisements.

Botnets
- Bots perform automated tasks; malicious bots form botnets for DDoS attacks and spam.
- Controlled via Internet Relay Chat (IRC) or web servers, botnets can consist of thousands of compromised computers.

Logic Bombs
- Execute malicious code when specific conditions are met, such as user actions or times.

Trojan Horses
- Programs disguised as legitimate software, often carry out malicious actions in the background.
- Remote Access Trojans (RATs) enable remote system control and are hidden in mobile code.
- **Crimeware Toolkits**
  - GUI-based kits for creating custom malware sold on the black market, lowering the entry barrier for cybercriminals.

Antimalware Software
- Uses signatures, heuristics, virtual machines, and behavior blockers for detection.
- Newer methods include reputation-based protection.

Spam Detection
- Spam emails are unsolicited junk emails that not only annoy recipients but also consume network bandwidth and pose malware threats.

- Bayesian filtering is a technique used to detect spam by applying statistical modeling to the words in an email message, analyzing their frequency and relationship to determine if it is spam.

- Spammers often manipulate email content to evade spam filters by misspelling words or using symbols, highlighting the constant battle between spammers and anti-spam measures.

Anti-malware Programs
- Anti-malware software requires administrative, physical, and technical controls.
- Organizations need a specific antimalware policy or one integrated into a broader security policy.
- Standards for the type and configuration of antimalware and antispyware software must be set.
- **Key practices include:**
  - Installing antimalware software on all devices.
  - Automating malware signature updates.
  - Preventing users from disabling antimalware software.
  - Having a predefined malware eradication process and contact person.
  - Automatically scanning external disks and backup files.
  - Reviewing antimalware policies and procedures annually.
  - Ensuring boot malware protection is provided by antimalware software.
  - Conducting antimalware scanning at network gateways and on all devices.
  - Automating and scheduling virus scans, not relying on manual scans.
  - Physically protecting critical systems against the local installation of malicious software.
  - Implementing antimalware solutions at network entry points, such as mail servers, proxies, or firewalls, is common.
  - Scanning software at these points looks for malware in specific protocols like SMTP, HTTP, and FTP, but not all incoming traffic, necessitating device-level antimalware protection.

Assessing the Security of Acquired Software
- Organizations often acquire software due to the impracticality of in-house development, which raises security concerns.
- Risk management processes should evaluate the impact of software behaving improperly, which could be due to defects or misconfiguration.
- Considerations include the type of information at risk, such as PII, intellectual property, or national security information.
- Vendor assessment is crucial, focusing on their reputation, patching regularity, and the potential risks associated with their software's market presence.
- Ideally, source code is available for internal code reviews, vulnerability assessments, and penetration testing.
- If in-house assessments are not possible, external penetration testing may be warranted, especially for high-risk scenarios.
- To mitigate risks of untested acquired software, organizations deploy it in specific subnetworks, apply hardened configurations, and monitor IDS/IPS rules.
- Functionality and controls can be adjusted over time as the software proves to be trustworthy.

Mind Map

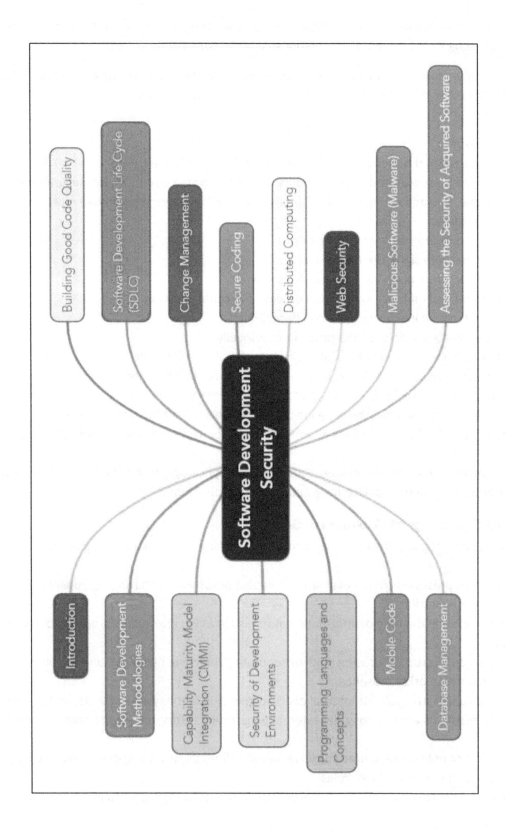

Made in United States
Orlando, FL
20 October 2024

52907613R00085